Fountai

A History of East Africa

Benson Okello

Fountain Publishers

Fountain Publishers Ltd
Kampala
P.O. 488
Kampala - Uganda
E-mail:fountain@starcom.co.ug
Web:www.fountainpublishers.com

© Benson Okello 2002
First published 2002

All rights resrved. No part of this publication may be reproduced, stored in retrieval system or transmitted in any form or by any means electronic, mechanical, photocopying, recording or otherwise without the prior written permission of the publisher.

ISBN   9970-02-277-6

Contents

Preface viii

Acknowledgements ix

1. Migration and settlement 1
General reasons for migration 1
Migration and settlement of the Cushites 2
The origin, movement and settlement of the Nilotes 2
The Jie 4
Reasons for migration of Teso people from Karamoja 4
River Lake Nilotes: The Luo 5
Origin, migration and settlement of Bantu 10
Revision 1 11

2. Cultivation and pastoralism in early East African societies 12
Revision 2 13

3. East African coast before 1500 15
Indian Ocean trade 15
The coastal towns and cities 16
Revision 3 20

4. Islam in East Africa 21
The rise of Swahili culture 22
Revision 4 23

5. East African coast 1498-1800 24
The Portuguese in East Africa 24
East African coast under Portuguese rule 28
Revision 5 30

6. The establishment of Omani power 32
Reasons for the delay in the establishment of Omani rule at the coast 32

iii

The Mazruis 33
Revision 6 36

7. Some interlacustrine kingdoms 37
Bunyoro Kitara 37
The Bachwezi 39
The Babito dynasty 42
Karagwe Empire 44
Nkore 47
Revision 7 48

8. Buganda 50
Origin 50
The growth of Buganda 50
Factors responsible for the rise and expansion of
Buganda kingdom 51
Political organisation 52
Social organisation 52
Economic organisation 53
Military organisation 54
Revision 8 54

9. Other East African peoples 56
The Nyamwezi 56
Organisation of Ntemi chiefdom 56
The Nandi (1500 - 1800) 57
The Maasai 59
The Kwavi 61
The Chagga 64
The Kikuyu 65
The Hehe 68
Revision 9 69

10. The Ngoni invasion of East Africa 70
Reasons for the Ngoni migration 70
The course of their migration 70
Ngoni in Ufipa Plateau 71

Reasons for Ngoni success 72
Consequences of Ngoni invasion of East Africa 73
Revision 10 74

11. Some notable East African leaders 76
Mirambo 76
Nyungu ya Mawe 78
Munyigumba 80
The rule of Mkwawa 80
Revision 11 81

12. Internal trade in East Africa 82
Long-distance trade 82
Trade routes 83
The participants in long-distance trade 84
Trade in Buganda 90
Revision 12 91

13. Slave trade in East Africa 92
Reasons for the intensification of slave trade
(18th - 19th centuries) 92
How the slaves were obtained 94
The Khartoumers 95
The impact of slave trade on the people of East Africa 96
The abolition of slave trade 97
Steps taken to abolish slave trade in East Africa 98
Revision 13 101

14. European missionaries and explorers in East Africa 102
Missionaries 102
Travellers or explorers in East Africa 105
Penetration of the interior of East Africa from Egypt 110
Problems of explorers 111
Christian missionaries in Buganda 112
Why missionary work thrived in Uganda 113
The relationship between Mwanga and the
missionaries 114

The results of missionary work in East Africa 116
Revision 14 118

15. European traders in East Africa 119
Trading companies in East Africa 119
The relationship between IBEA Co and other
companies at the East African coast 121
Problems faced by the trading companies 122
Imperialists 123
Revision 15 125

16. The scramble for and partition of East Africa 126
Egyptian imperialism 126
The European scramble for and partition of
East Africa (1884 - 1900) 128
The Berlin Conference 130
Revision 16 131

17. British conquest and occupation of Uganda
(1884 - 1914) 133
Captain Lugard and Buganda 133
Lugard's expedition in western Uganda 134
Lugard's achievements in western Uganda 135
Lugard returns to Buganda 135
Buganda Agreement 136
Terms of Buganda Agreement 137
Toro Agreement, 1900 140
Ankole Agreement of 1901 140
The extension of British rule to Bunyoro 141
The extension of colonial rule to eastern Uganda 141
Extension of colonial rule in northern Uganda 144
Revision 17 146

18. Reactions to the establishment of colonial rule in
Uganda 148
Apollo Kagwa 148

Nuwa Mbaguta 149
Kabalega of Bunyoro 151
Rwot Awich 153
Revision 18 154

19. British conquest of Kenya 155
Reactions to the establishment of colonial rule in
Kenya 156
Revision 19 159

20. German East Africa (Tanganyika) 160
Tanganyika under German East Africa Company's
administration 161
Establishment of German colonial rule in
Tanganyika 164
Revision 20 166

21. Zanzibar and the British (1900-1914) 167
Political, economic and constitutional developments in
Zanzibar after First World War 168

22. The building of Uganda Railway 170
Reasons for construction of Uganda Railway 170
The construction of Uganda Railway 171
Effects of Uganda Railway 173

23. British indirect rule in Uganda 174
Origin of indirect rule 174
Reasons for indirect rule 174
Administrative structure of indirect rule 175
Problems met by British administrators before 1914 177
Revision 21,22 & 23 178

24. German administration in Tanganyika up to 1914.... 180
The Maji Maji uprising (1905 - 1907) 181
Revision 24 185

vii

25. The First World War and its effects 187
How the war was fought in East Africa 187
Effects of the First World War in East Africa 188

26. Economic and social development of Tanganyika (1900 - 1963) 190
Transport and trade 191
Development of education and towns up to 1914 191
Before 1945 192
After 1945 193
Education before 1945 194
Education after 1945 194
Revision 25 & 26 195

27. Economic and social development of Uganda (1900-63) 197
Economic development in Uganda before 1920 197
Health 199
Economic development before 1945 199
Between 1946 and 1963 200
Education 201

28. Economic and social development of Kenya (1900 - 1963) 206
Economic development of Kenya between 1920 and 1945 207
Between 1945 and 1963 208
Education in Kenya 208
Revision 27 & 28 210

29. Uganda's constitutional development (1906 - 1963) ... 212

30. Uganda's political development (1906 - 1962) 216
Reasons for nationalist movements in Uganda 217
The development of political parties in Uganda 218

viii

31. Tanganyika's constitutional development (1918 - 1961) 222
Constitutional development: before 1945 222

32. Political development in Tanganyika (1918-1961) 226
Political development after 1945 227

33. Constitutional development in Kenya (1900 - 1963) ... 231
Constitutional development after First World War 231
Constitutional development after Second World War 233

34 Political development in Kenya 235
Asians 235
Africans 236
Mau Mau rebellion 239

35. Closer union in East Africa 245
Uganda 245
Kenya 245
Tanganyika 246
Formation of East Africa High Commission 247
Functions of the Commission 247
Revision 29, 30, 31, 32, 33, 34 & 35 248

Index 251

Preface

This book is intended to guide O level students preparing to sit History of East Africa Paper 241/1. The book can also be of relevance to A level students who are preparing to sit Paper 210/6, History of Africa from 1855 to 1914, because of its wide coverage of the topics taught in the history of the region.

The book was written in order to help alleviate the shortage of textbooks on East African history in many schools. It is hoped that history teachers will find this book useful since the author follows the history syllabus closely and logically. It can also help someone with no prior knowledge of the History of East Africa.

I have endeavoured to write the book in simple and straightforward language so that it can be read, understood and digested by students without the help of their teachers.

Benson Okello

Acknowledgements

"No man is an island unto himself" is a saying which comes readily to mind when one is developing work of this kind. I owe a lot of gratitude to members of my family, Mrs Grace Okello and my sons Dan, Solomon and Isaac, for tolerating my frequent absences from home during the period of research.

I would also like to thank my friends, especially Mr Ajore, Miss M. Matama, Miss Christine Apolot , Miss Rose Munyira, Miss Kwambuka (deceased), Mr O. Kadokech and all other members of the History Department whose unwavering encouragement kept me going until the moment my publisher thought the book was good enough for publication.

I also thank my former teachers, especially the late D.H. Okwir, formerly of Comboni College, Lira; my University lecturers, especially Professor P.G. Okoth, Mr G. Asiimwe, Professor B. Akiiki, Professor J.C. Ssekamwa and many others whose academic guidance made me who I am today.

Finally, I should like to thank Mrs S.R. Oloka and Mrs V. Wabwire who typed the manuscript.

1

Migration and settlement

The word *migration* comes from the verb *to migrate* which means to move from one place to another. The movement of different stocks of people into East Africa was a very long process which took over two thousand years. It was therefore a very slow process, with people coming in small numbers, usually in small family groups, not as whole tribes.

Movement during the migrations was sometimes seasonal. This seasonal movement is referred to as *transhumance*. The Luo people were well known for practising transhumance.

It is worth noting that physical features such as mountains played a prominent role in the lives of the migrants as they were used as reference points for dispersal and convergence.

General reasons for migration

Several reasons were responsible for the migration of several groups into East Africa.

Famine: This is believed to be one of the major causes of migration of the early peoples into East Africa. As famine struck, people preferred moving to new places where they could get wild fruits and tubers to eat and also where they could carry out cultivation.

Drought: This was also responsible for the migration of many tribes into East Africa. These tribes came to look for places where water was available. This is especially true of the farmers and the nomads as they had to look for places with rain and water for their crops and animals.

Overpopulation: As the population of a place grew larger, dispersal would take place as people searched for free land for settlement.

Political oppression: Whenever their leaders oppressed them, people would take refuge in other places.

Tribal conflicts: This might also have encouraged migration as tribes which were weaker would run away from stronger ones.

Migration and settlement of the Cushites

The Cushites constitute a branch of the Caucasoid race which includes the Western Asians, Arabs and Europeans. These people in East Africa include the Somali, Galla and the Boran. They are believed to have come from Arabia. They moved through the Horn of Africa and from there spread to Ethiopia and Somalia.

The Cushites however were not in any way related to the ancient kingdom of Cush. The Cushites who moved into East Africa were referred to as the Southern Cushites. They occupied the plains and highlands of Kenya and northern Tanzania. It is estimated that the Cushites entered Kenya in about 1000 B.C. They were probably food producers who seemed to have had knowledge of the use of modern irrigation for farming. It is believed that the Galla came first, followed by the Somali, and that they probably came into contact with the Bantu who stopped them from moving farther south.

Finally, they had to settle in north-eastern Kenya. They proceeded to intermarry with other groups and most of them lost their characteristics to those tribes with whom they intermarried. However, some remnants of the Cushites who have the distinctive characteristics of the early migrants have survived to date. These are Iraqw, Dahalo and Mbugu.

The Cushites' historical burial site was discovered by Dr Leakey at the Njoro River cave.

According to some historians, the legendary Chwezi might have descended in some way from the Cushites, although this view is disputed by modern historians.

Some Cushites, such as the Galla, played a very big role in disrupting life within the area they occupied.

The origin, movement and settlement of the Nilotes

The Nilotes are a purely linguistic classification of a very large group which has been divided into three major branches.

These three branches are: the Highland Nilotes, Plains Nilotes and River Lake Nilotes.

The Highland Nilotes are the Kalenjin group of tribes. The Plains Nilotes include the Maasai and the River Lake Nilotes are the Luo.

The Plains Nilotes include the Maasai, Turkana, Iteso, Karimojong, Pokot, Samburu, Nandi and Kipsigis. Like the Bantu, the Plains Nilotes are believed to have descended from Negro stock. They are believed to have originated from the southern border of the Ethiopian highlands at various times during the first millennium AD. The Plains Nilotes were predominantly a pastoral group whose livelihood depended on their animals.

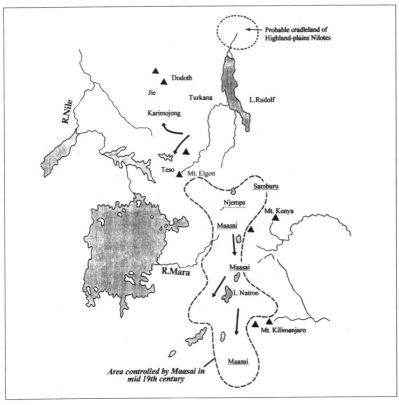

Plains Nilotes: Movements and settlement in East Africa

The Jie

The Jie group comprises the Karimojong, Kumam, Turkana, the Jie and Iteso. The Langi may also be included in this group although many people believe that they had some Luo relations.

Though their origin is not well known, it is believed that the Jie came from the Suk hills close to the current Karamoja area. Meanwhile, some historians believe that they might have come either from Ethiopia or Sudan.

The ancestors of these people first settled in present-day Karamoja district before they dispersed and emigrated to their present areas. However, the Teso people migrated from Karamoja towards the end of the 17th century or the beginning of the 18th century and settled in their present-day land in eastern Uganda.

Reasons for migration of Teso people from Karamoja

Several reasons are responsible for the migration of the Teso people from Karamoja.

Overstocking: They probably migrated from Karamoja owing to overstocking. They had a lot of cattle and they could not continue living together with the Karimojong in one place.

Lack of water: This was another possible reason. There was need to find enough water for both their own consumption and for their animals.

Lack of grazing land: They were looking for a better place to graze their animals.

Overpopulation: People had to move away in search of places that were free from population pressure.

Internal and external conflicts: These might also have triggered their movement away from Karamoja. The Karimojong and Turkana might have been raiding them frequently.

Famine: This was another possible cause of Teso migration from Karamoja, especially the famine of Laparanat which forced many people to move away to look for food.

Results of Teso migration

As a result of their migration, the Iteso acquired iron hoes through bartering with the Langi and they became farmers in addition to being pastoralists.

They also acquired new crops like sweet potatoes and groundnuts. Because of this, the Teso people, unlike their relatives the Karimojong, built houses where they could stay permanently. Their population increased rapidly due to the abundance of food which they were producing with the hoes they had acquired.

River Lake Nilotes: The Luo

The Luo are believed to have originated from southern Sudan in the region of Bar-el-Ghazel. This might have been their cradleland. From Bahr-el-Ghazel, the Luo moved to Wipac where they split into three main groups. One of the groups went northwards and formed the present-day tribes of Shilluk, Nuer and the Dinka. Meanwhile another group went towards the southern border of Ethiopia and Sudan where they became known as the Anuak. The third group followed the course of the Nile and settled at a place called Pubungu in present-day Pakwach in Uganda.

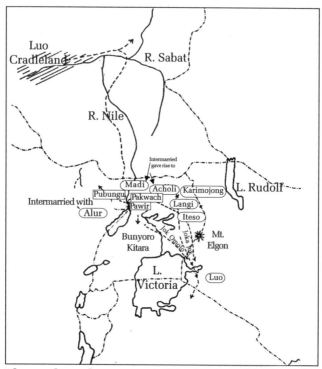

The southward movement of the Luo-speaking peoples

At Pubungu, a quarrel broke out between two brothers, Labongo and Gipir (Nyipir). In order to avoid further conflict, Gipir moved across the River Nile and settled in the present-day West Nile districts with his followers. His group intermarried with the Sudanic Madi, Okebo and Lendu. Their inter-marriages gave rise to the present Alur sub-group of the Luo people.

The second group of the Luo people was led by Labongo, who went southwards towards Pawir or Chope in Bunyoro. Here they founded the Bito line of rulers. Later this Pawir group expanded into Acholi, Lango and Alur.

A third group is believed to have stayed at Pubungu and later moved eastwards to Budama (present-day Tororo district) and Kenya. Their descendants are believed to be the Jopadhola and the Kenyan Luo. The Luo group which went to Acholi from Pawir is believed to have been led by Jok-Omolo. This group also passed through some parts of Lango. The group which went to Budama was led by Adhola. This group passed through southern Lango to Kaberamaido, and the rest went to the south of present-day Busoga and lived there for about three generations.

Some of the Jok-Omolo Luo joined the Luo in Busoga. From there, part of the group went to Budama around present-day Tororo. There they became known as Jopadhola (meaning the people of Adhola). Meanwhile, those who remained in Busoga formed an ethnic group called Balamogi.

Jok-Ajok led the first group to the Ramogi hills in Nyanza Province in Kenya. Their settlement covered both sides of the Ramogi hills and present-day Uyoma, Seme, Nyakach and Alega areas. The Jok-Omolo group later passed through Samia and Bunyala and spread to Gem, southern Nyanza, Ugeinya and Alego. The Jok-Owiny group covered other areas of southern Nyanza, Alego and Kadimo.

Effects of Luo migration in East Africa
The movement of the Luo from Bahr-el-Ghazel to East Africa had far-reaching political, economic and social effects in East Africa.

- Their migration led to the effective settlement of Lango, Acholi and West Nile.

- The Luo became rulers while the local people were commoners.

- The Luo founded many chiefdoms in East Africa, e.g. Koc Ragem in the lowlands of Alur, Ukuru in the highlands, and Patiko in Acholi.

- Their migration also led to the disintegration of Chwezi rule.

- The Luo established the Babito ruling dynasty in Bunyoro.

- They also established sub-dynasties in Buganda, Ankole, Rwanda, Kiziba, Busoga, etc.

- Kingdoms which were not founded by the Luo copied the Luo system, e.g. Payera, Atyak, Ajali, all in East and West Acholi.

- The Luo introduced the hereditary system of kingship with the drum as part of the royal regalia.

- They founded small states in Busoga, e.g. Bukooli, Kigulu and Luwaka.

- They waged a lot of wars which led to the death of people. This was typical of the Luo of Nyanza in Kenya. They fought the Maasai, Nandi and Abaluhya.

- The Luo contributed a lot in the peopling of East Africa, e.g. the inhabitants of northern Uganda (Acholi, Langi and Alur) are the descendants of the Luo.

- Their language was adopted and used by other tribes, e.g. by Luo Abasuba, Langi, etc. The Luo Abasuba were the destitutes who had run away from their tribes to seek protection from the Luo people but were assimilated by the Luo.

- The Luo also brought with them knowledge of farming. They grew millet, sorghum and leguminous crops. All these were adopted.

- They formed new societies like Kumam, Langi and Alur through inter-marriages with the people they encountered during the course of their migration.

- They were responsible for the development of new customs and cultures in East Africa.

A group of Acholi chiefs

Origin, migration and settlement of Bantu

The term Bantu refers to the people who speak the language referred to as 'ntu'. Like the Nilotes, the Bantu are Negroes who speak different languages. Their cradleland is believed to have been around the River Congo area. Historians believe that the Bantu migrated from their cradleland about two thousand years ago and moved up to the area around the Katonga region in the Democratic Republic of Congo, where they dispersed again. The Bantu are believed to have entered East Africa from the west in around 1000 - 1500 AD.

There were about four groups of the Bantu who entered East Africa. These were: the Highland and Coastal Bantu, the Western Tanzania Bantu, The Central and Southern Tanzania Bantu, and the interlacustrine (or western) Bantu. According to oral traditions, the Highland and Coastal Bantu migrated into East Africa from the south-eastern direction. Their place of dispersal is believed to be the coastal Shungwaya area.

The Bantu group which dispersed from the coastal Shungwaya area include the Meru, Pare, Shambaa, Chagga and Kikuyu. Meanwhile, the migration of the Western Tanzania Bantu is believed to have been closely linked with the Central African Bantu expansion. They entered East Africa from the south-western direction and occupied the areas where they are found today.

The migration of the Central and Southern Tanzania Bantu into East Africa was also closely linked with the movements of the Bantu of Central Africa. This group consisted of the Gogo, Pogoro, Yao, Mwera and Makonde. Furthermore the migration of the interlascustrine or Western Bantu was from the western direction into East Africa. They established some flourishing communities around the lakes of East Africa. This group includes the Banyarwanda, Banyankore, Baganda, Banyoro and Abaluhya.

The Ngoni conquest and settlement of East Africa in the 19th century was the last wave of the Bantu migration into East Africa.

All these migrants did not enter East Africa as the tribes of today, but the present-day East African tribes emerged later as a result of assimilation of various groups of people with diverse cultures.

Revision 1

1 (a) Describe the movement and settlement of the Eastern Bantu into East Africa up to AD 1800.

  (b) How were the Cushitic peoples affected by their movement and settlement?

2 (a) Why did the Bantu move into East Africa?

  (b) Describe their migration and settlement in East Africa before 1800.

3 (a) Why did the Luo migrate from their cradleland (initial homeland)?

  (b) What were the results of their migration?

4 (a) Why did the Iteso migrate from Karamoja in the 16th century?

  (b) Describe their migration and settlement in East Africa between 1500 - 1890.

2

Cultivation and pastoralism in early East African societies

The idea of cultivation and producing food is believed to have started in the Middle East, especially in Shandibar in the northern part of present-day Iraq.

Through the scientific process known as carbon 14 dating, archaeologists have determined that food production probably started in Shandibar in approximately 9000 BC. Other evidence was found at Tell es Sultan, the site of present-day Jericho. Here food production is thought to have started in about 8000 BC. From those historical sites, the idea of farming or cultivation and pastoralism spread to other parts of the world.

The idea of cultivation and pastoralism came to the African continent through Egypt. At Fayum in the Nile Delta the idea of keeping or rearing goats, cattle, sheep as well as fishing dates to around 6000 BC. This civilisation therefore spread along the Nile valley and by around 1500 BC, knowledge of cultivation and pastoralism had already reached East Africa, but the influence stayed minimal until around 500 AD.

The skills of cultivation and pastoralism were passed on to other people through migration and personal contact with neighbours. As such both cultivators and pastoralists had to learn by trial and error what would adapt best to their respective climates. The crops which were very important were wheat and barley which were grown in North Africa; sorghum, millet, eleusine and crops better suited to the hotter tropical areas, especially areas south of the Sahara. In wet regions, especially around the lakes, other crops like bananas, rice and certain yams were grown. In East Africa, bananas, rice, yams and sweet potatoes were introduced along the Indian Ocean trade routes about two hundred years ago. Millet and sorghum were brought from the Ethiopian highlands about three to four thousand years ago. Maize and cassava were introduced to East Africa from the Americas.

The first domestic cattle, sheep and goats were brought into north-eastern Africa from western Asia and later on reached East Africa. As people acquired the skills of cultivation and animal keeping (rearing), there arose a need to settle down and stop subsisting on fruit as had been the case during the Stone Age. The banana cultivators settled in fertile areas, especially around the lake shores, and the herdsmen settled on the plains where they could easily graze their animals.

As two distinct groups of farmers and cattle keepers developed, trade ensued between them since each group needed the products of the other. However, the quantity and the quality of food produced depended on the climate and on land use. Agriculture and grazing tended to exhaust the land very fast. What the early people in East Africa did, therefore, was to practise shifting cultivation and movement of livestock from pasture to pasture. Agriculture and cultivation in particular improved a great deal when iron-working started in East Africa. There was a great improvement on the tools used. Man shifted from the use of stone tools to the use of iron implements.

The population of East Africa grew rapidly as the production of food increased owing to the introduction of new implements. Food items like bananas, millet, sorghum, yams and cassava were already being produced around five hundred years before. Examples of the pastoralists or cattle keepers in East Africa were the Bachwezi and the Iteso group (Karimojong, Teso, Turkana, Maasai, etc.) while the rest were farmers.

Revision 2

1. What was the contribution of food crops to the development of early humans in East Africa?
2. With examples show how various food crops were brought to East Africa.

3. Why did early humans in East Africa practise shifting cultivation?
4. What was the contribution of agriculture to the lives of early humans in East Africa?
5. (a) From which part of the world did livestock, especially cattle, originate?
   (b) Who were the pastoralists in East Africa before the time of colonialism?
6. Where did food production begin and in which year?

3

East African coast before 1500

Indian Ocean trade

Today, coastal history is better known to historians than the history of the interior. This is because the early trade which connected East Africa to the outside world attracted many Greek traders. These traders took pains to write down its history in the famous guide book known as the *Periplus of the Erythraean Sea*. We do not know the authors of this guide book. Trade between the coast of East Africa and other parts of the world across the Indian Ocean is believed to have started in the second half of the first century AD.

The *Periplus* was, therefore, written to guide the traders, especially to many cities including Rhapta, which has not yet been located. The coast of East Africa was called Azania by those writers.

Items of early trade

According to our only source of information, i.e. the *Periplus of the Erythraean Sea*, the trade between the Arab sailors and the people of the coast of East Africa involved the following items: ivory, palm oil, tortoise shells, rhinoceros horns, cinnamon, slaves and frankinsence.

All those items were obtained from the East African people. It was noted by another prominent writer, Ptolemy, in the second century that the above items were the most important commodities of this early coastal trade. Among those who came to East Africa to trade by sea were the Ancient Greeks, Egyptians and Arabs.

Trade in ivory and gold was carried on chiefly with the ports of Oman and Siraf. Imported articles included glass, iron tools, wine and wheat and these were often used as gifts. By the beginning of the fifth century the Arabs had dominated the coastal zone as their trading area, and from around 420-439 AD, East African trade was firmly in the hands of the Persians. They often referred to the coast as the land of the Zenj, meaning the land of the black people.

As a result of the life and teachings of Mohammed (570-632 AD), Islam as a new religion and its civilisation spread widely in the Middle East. Its followers established an empire that stretched from the Atlantic coast of North Africa and Spain to the eastern shore of the Indian Ocean.

This religion had a far-reaching commercial and political effect on the people of East Africa during the trans-Indian ocean trade. It also strengthened the link between the coastal peoples with Arabia, Persian Gulf and India.

But when Prophet Mohammed died in 632 AD, quarrels broke out in those areas which had an Islamic influence as people wanted to get a leader who would replace Mohammed. In the confusion that ensued, many people came to East Africa to settle in about 690 AD.

Between 690 AD and 1000 AD, the Arabs and Persians built about 38 cities at the coast of East Africa. These cities were built between Mogadishu and Kilwa. All the above cities were quite separate from one another. Each city had its own sultan and code of law. The cities were mostly hostile to one another. For instance Mombasa was hostile to Nairobi.

As noted before, these cities were located in the Zenj empire. This was an empire without an emperor and, furthermore, it was a multi-racial settlement with people whose various cultures were only harmonised by the Kiswahili language and Islam.

The coastal towns and cities

Most of the towns were situated on the peninsulas of islands of East Africa. There was a marked difference between the people of the towns and the people from the hinterland. Most of the towns had rulers who claimed descent from the Arab and Persian ruling classes. Those rulers would govern with the help of a small advisory council. Each of the council officials had specific tasks to perform. For instance, the

Muhtasib was in charge of administration and the Khadi was in charge of the courts and Shariah law. Shariah law was the guiding principle for the administrators.

The most outstanding coastal towns were Kilwa and Mogadishu during the early years of settlement of the East African coast. Later, however, their position was challenged by towns such as Pate and Mombasa.

Mogadishu

It was by far the largest of all the towns situated on the Benadir coast. It is also believed that this great town was the first to rise and prosper among all the coastal towns.

Mogadishu was founded in the 11th century, and by the 13th century it had become the most prosperous of all the towns. It soon became a port of call for all dhows coming south along the coast due to its nearness to the northern trade route. The rulers of the city were referred to as Sheikhs and they lived in luxury as they possessed a lot of wealth.

However, Mogadishu lost control of the trade in gold from Sofala and began to decline seriously. Yet between the 10th and 15th centuries, it was second only to Kilwa. By the 15th century, almost all the people living in Mogadishu were Muslims. No coastal town boasted a larger number of converts than Mogadishu. Mogadishu had very little to do with the other coastal towns, but had contacts with the Arab world.

Kilwa

From the beginning of the 14th century, Kilwa was the most prosperous town on the coast of East Africa. It is believed that the Persians established it in the early 13th century under their new ruler from the Shirazi dynasty. The Shirazi rulers came from the Benadir coast.

Kilwa first rose to prominence under the leadership of Ali Ibn-al-Hassan who changed Kilwa from a small trading centre into a big commercial centre with a strong fortress. He raided northwards along the coast and brought many small areas under his influence, including Pemba. Protected from invaders by its fortress, Kilwa became an absolute controller of the gold trade of East Africa. The town was therefore referred to as Kilwa Kisiwani.

In about 1270, Al-Hassan Ibn Sulaiman I started to build the Great Mosque at Kilwa in a bid to promote Islam at the coast of East Africa. A palace was built in Kilwa about 1320, and archaeologists believe that the palace was the biggest building south of the Sahara at that time. The palace is commonly referred to as Husuni Kubwa. Many other fine buildings were erected, the greatest of them being the Great Mosque. It was built using Arab architecture.

Kilwa was inhabited by Swahili and Arab peoples.

However, by 1490 Kilwa had seriously declined owing to wars in the interior which interrupted the flow of gold from Sofala.

Mombasa

Mombasa was founded probably in the 12th century as an export centre for slaves and ivory. It remained a small settlement until the second half of the 15th century when it gradually grew rich. The expansion and prosperity of Mombasa town was due to the expansion of the Indian Ocean trade. By 1490, Mombasa had grown into a prosperous city with a fortified wall around it. The buildings in Mombasa could easily rival those of Kilwa in terms of their fineness and beauty. Mombasa was so prosperous that it was capable of putting up very serious resistance to the Portuguese invaders in the 15th century.

Mombasa had been visited by many Muslim traders like Al Idrisi in the 12th century and Ibn Batuta in 1331. The inhabitants of Mombasa were warlike and were determined not to surrender their independence to the Portuguese who had come in full force to try to subject them to colonial rule. However, Ibn Batuta described the inhabitants of Mombasa as being very pious and honourable.

Although the rulers of Mombasa were Arabs, the culture of Mombasa had a very strong traditional African element.

Fort Jesus in Mombasa

Zanzibar

Zanzibar and Pemba were among the first places to be settled by foreigners. Historians believe that the earliest known trading post, Qanbalu, was probably on Pemba Island. Zanzibar was ruled by Arabs who established their supremacy over the local people of the island. Because of their rule, Zanzibar became a very free trading centre.

Zanzibar was independent of Kilwa, and its people could not allow foreigners to interfere in their affairs. The economy of Zanzibar grew in the 15th century. Their rulers or sultans minted their own coins.

Malindi

Malindi was founded around the 12th century as a mere trading post. It was situated near Mombasa and as a result there was always very serious rivalry between the two towns. Although Malindi was also well positioned, it could not match Mombasa in strength and was therefore always willing to ally itself with anybody in an attempt to destroy Mombasa. Malindi also embraced Islam and its rulers took the title of Sultan. However, many of its traditional customs were preserved. The people of Malindi learned new ways of government and administration from the Arabs. The inhabitants of Malindi were Africans and Swahili people.

Revision 3

1. (a) Describe the trading activities between the East African coast and Asia up to 1500 AD.

   (b) How were the coastal peoples affected by this trade?

2. (a) Describe the trade on the East African coast before 1500.

   (b) What were the results?

3. (a) What did the Greek term 'Azania' refer to?

   (b) Describe a trade relationship between Azania and Asia between 1000 and 1500 AD.

4. (a) Which were the principal centres of power and wealth on the East African coast between 1200 and 1500 AD?

   (b) Describe the organisation of the East African coastal trade up to 1500 AD.

4

Islam in East Africa

The newcomers to the East African coast, as noted before, were the Arabs and Persians. These people had already been influenced by the life and teachings of Prophet Mohammed (AD 570-632). Islam did not only develop into a political and military system, but it also gave rise to the revival of learning. Literature and science, architecture and art, law and philosophy blossomed in the universities and centres of learning throughout the Muslim world.

In East Africa ,therefore, Islam brought about a revolution. This revolution had a profound effect which continues to be felt to this day. This effect was far-reaching politically, economically and socially.

Politically, Islam fostered unity and tranquillity in East Africa. People of diverse cultures got united under one Muslim leader in both small and bigger settlements such as Kilwa, Mogadishu, Mombasa, etc. Trade boomed between the East African coastal towns and the outside world.

The countries involved in this Indian Ocean trade included Persia, Egypt, India, Burma, China and Thailand. The main items of the trade were slaves, ivory, rhinoceros horns, tortoise shells, cowrie shells, swords, ironware, glassware, gold, etc. Islam therefore facilitated the growth of the East African coastal towns.

Furthermore, the Islamic laws were used in the administration and running of the day-to-day affairs of the coastal towns. Mosques were built. These were places for adoring Allah (God), and also where moral standards based on Islamic principles were imparted to people.

Teachers of the Islamic religion, the Qadis, received training for their job. Their work was to teach the coastal peoples and convert them to Islam. Education also flourished at the coast during this time. Koranic schools were built where reading of the Koran was taught. It was not only the Koran that was taught, but other subjects like history, music, poetry and Arab literature. Arab culture was also adopted wholesale. All the coastal peoples began to wear caps, turbans and sandals like the Arabs.

As a result, the building of durable houses with sun-baked bricks and stones was adopted by the people of the East African coast. This raised the standard of living of the coastal peoples.

Interestingly, the Arabs, Persians and others who settled at the coast of East Africa mixed freely with the Africans and in the process they intermarried. In the long run, their products emerged into a people of a different culture commonly referred to as the Swahili people. A new language also emerged. This was Kiswahili, which is a mixture of Bantu, Arab and Persian words.

Because of the above influences the East African coast had developed so much that when the Portuguese arrived there, they were immensely impressed with its prosperity. In fact they mistook it for Saudi Arabia. They therefore started planning how to take permanent control of it.

The rise of Swahili culture

The name *Swahili* is derived from the Arabic word 'Swahili' meaning coasts. Contact between the East African coast and Arabia was made as early as the 1st century AD. However, the earliest settlement known is believed to have been at Pate which was founded in about 687 AD.

During the next 600 years, other cities like Lamu, Malindi, Mombasa and Kilwa were founded and they reached a very high level of civilisation until they were invaded by the Portuguese in the 16th century. By 1832, Swahili culture had become very distinct.

Revision 4

1. (a) Why did the Arabs settle along the East African coast between AD 1000 and 1500?

    (b) What influence did their settlement have on the coastal Bantu during that period?

2. What were the results of Islam in East Africa?

5

East African coast 1498-1800

The Portuguese in East Africa

The Portuguese were the first people to search for a sea route to India. Their leaders had been yearning to find a way round the continent of Africa. Their ambition was fulfilled when a Portuguese navigator, Vasco da Gama, sailed up the East African coast in 1497 on his way to India.

It is worth noting that at the coast of East Africa, the Portuguese were rivals of the Arabs who were also well armed as a means of protecting their commercial interests. The cause of this rivalry dates back to about 711 AD when the Arabs conquered Portugal and the Iberian peninsula, forcibly converted the natives to Islam and ruled them for a very long time. The natives had to be assisted by some Christian countries to dislodge the Arabs. By the time they came to East Africa, therefore, the Portuguese harboured a lot of anger against the Arabs and their religion, Islam.

The Portuguese had fought and successfully defeated some Arab settlements around Portugal. Encouraged by this initial success, they wanted to destroy Islam right at its cradle in Saudi Arabia. Instead they ended up in East Africa, entirely by accident.

Reasons for Portuguese conquest of East African coast

The Portuguese conquered the coastal part of East Africa for strategic, economic and social reasons. From the strategic viewpoint, the Portuguese wanted a place like East Africa which had a lot of harbours and inlets along the coast. The Portuguese also realised that the East African coast was situated mid-way between India and Portugal.

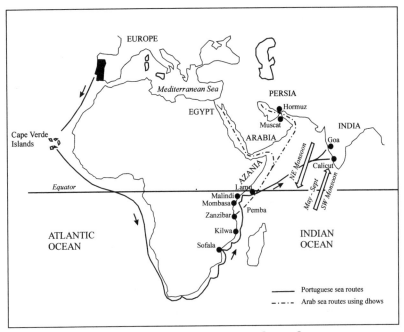

Portuguese and Arab sea routes in the 16th century

They would, therefore, stop and pick up water and food supplies on their way to India from East Africa. They considered the coast of East Africa suitable for stationing their vessels to protect their merchant ships. They also thought that with East Africa being their stronghold, no one would be able to interfere with their commercial activities there.

They also believed that East Africa was very strategic as they would be able to pre-empt and stop their rivals the Arabs, Egyptians and the Turks.

On the other hand, the Portuguese had an economic motive in conquering the East African coast. They wanted to share in the profits of the East African trade with the Arabs and other peoples. They also wanted to levy taxes on the traders who were coming to East Africa to buy lucrative items like gold from Sofala and ivory from the interior.

The Portuguese deeply hated the Arabs and their religion Islam. So their coming and conquest of East Africa was aimed at converting the Arabs to Christianity by force just as the

Arabs had forcibly converted them to Islam in 711 AD. They also wanted to have contact with the legendary Prester John who was believed to be a Christian king ruling in the north-eastern part of Africa.

Another important reason for their conquest of East Africa was their hunger for exploration. Exploration was an idea which was very widespread in Europe after the 13th century owing to the Renaissance, i.e. the rebirth of knowledge. Europeans therefore wanted to discover their immediate environment and what lay beyond it to explore new possibilities for survival. In Portugal, this hunger for discovery was inspired by Henry the Navigator who sent out ship after ship to find out unknown lands. The desire for this knowledge went hand in hand with the desire for riches.

Portuguese conquest of East Africa

The conquest of East Africa and the eventual establishment of Portuguese rule started when Pedro Ivares Cabral launched an unsuccessful attack against Sofala in 1500.

In 1502, Vasco da Gama returned with a fleet of nineteen ships, carrying a large force of well armed soldiers, and attacked Kilwa which he thought was very important in gold trade. He defeated Sultan Ibrahim and imprisoned him. The Sultan was only released after he had acknowledged Portuguese supremacy and had accepted to pay tribute to Portugal.

In another attempt to conquer East Africa in 1503, Ruy Laurenco Ravasco forced the islands of Mafia and Zanzibar and many other, smaller coastal towns to pay tribute to Portugal and also to accept wholesale the overlordship of the king of Portugal.

In 1505, another adventurous Portuguese, Francisco d'Almeida, left Portugal for the coast of East Africa with a fleet of twenty ships and 1500 soldiers. He met a lot of resistance but he managed to capture Kilwa and Mombasa. He further subjected many towns and islands to Portuguese rule.

The towns which resisted Portuguese conquest were severely punished and stripped of all their valuable property, but those cities which did not resist were only forced to pay tribute. Examples of towns looted were Kilwa, Mombasa, Oja and Brava. By 1509, the entire East African coast had fallen to the Portuguese conquerors, whose sphere of influence now stretched from Sofala to Socotra.

Francisco d'Almeida, Portuguese Governor General

Reasons for the success of the Portuguese conquest of East Africa

Several factors were responsible for the Portuguese success in conquering the coast of East Africa. Firstly, the leaders were so disorganised and disunited that they could not come together to fight the common enemy, the Portuguese. For instance, the Sultan of Kilwa could not unite with the Sultan of Mombasa. Otherwise it would have been difficult for the Portuguese to conquer East Africa.

Secondly, the Portuguese had better armed and well trained soldiers at the coast. So they could overrun the towns easily. The weapons which the Portuguese possessed, for instance muskets which puffed smoke and made a terrifying noise, as well as killed people, sent fear down the spines of the Arabs who had only daggers as their weapons. To make it worse the daggers could not kill the Portuguese soldiers easily since they wore armour.

In addition to their superior weapons, the Portuguese soldiers were well supplied with food, compared to the hungry Arab warriors whose food supplies had been cut off.

East African coast under Portuguese rule

In 1509, after East Africa had fallen into the hands of the Portuguese, Alfonso d'Albuquerque, a Portuguese viceroy in India, made Goa his headquarters. Two captains were appointed to govern the East African coast. Cape Delgado was demarcated as the midpoint of the East African Portuguese possessions. The area south of Cape Delgado was placed under one captain and its headquarters was at Mozambique; while the northern area was placed under another captain and its headquarters was at Malindi.

These Portuguese captains together with their assistants kept law and order. They were also instructed to suppress any uprising by their subjects. The collection of taxes and tributes was also their duty. The collection of the taxes and tributes was carried out with a lot of harassment and brutality. The two captions were also supposed to submit reports on their administration to the viceroy in Goa.

During the two hundred years that the Portuguese ruled the East African coast, there was continuous decline. Nobody prospered, including the Portuguese themselves; towns decayed and movement of merchandise slowed down. All these setbacks can be attributed to the problems which the Portuguese administration faced in East Africa.

Problems faced by the Portuguese on the East African coast

The problems at the coast which eventually led to the decline and the collapse of Portuguese administration were many.
- The area under Portuguese control was too vast; it included 4000 kilometres of coast and highlands. This area was unmanageable and eventually the Portuguese failed to keep it intact.

- Only few Portuguese were willing to come to the coast of East Africa, which led to shortage of manpower.

- The few Portuguese administrators who came to the coast were only interested in money. Furthermore, they were very corrupt. This made their subjects very angry and they decided to rebel against the administrators.

- Tropical diseases like malaria caused a lot of fear among the Portuguese. Many of them did not want to come to the coast and many of those who did died of the disease.

- The mistreatment of the local people by the Portuguese officials who did not want to mix freely with Africans, caused enmity between them.

- Both Portugal and Spain were under the same administration. This union was detrimental to Portuguese colonial affairs in East Africa since the union mattered more than colonialism in East Africa.

- In the 17th century, the British and the Dutch entered the Indian Ocean trade and managed to break Portuguese monopoly. This greatly weakened the Portuguese since they were facing a greater force than that from East Africa. Many people in East Africa took advantage of the confusion and rebelled against the Portuguese.

- The Omani Arabs gave a lot of military assistance to the people of East Africa against the Portuguese who suffered heavy casualties when they were driven out in about 1668. They tried to return to Mombasa in 1728 but they were routed in 1729.

Results of Portuguese rule in East Africa
Portuguese rule at the coast of East Africa had both good and bad results.

Positive effects
- The Portuguese created a cordial relationship between the East African coast and India (Goa).

- The Portuguese made East Africa known to the outside world, especially Europe.

- The Portuguese introduced food crops such as cassava, maize, pineapples, groundnuts, sweet potatoes, pawpaws and guavas in East Africa.

- They also constructed Fort Jesus which later played a great role in the lives of East Africans.

- They also brought in many traders and craftsmen who were more modern than the Arabs.

Negative effects

- Trade and culture declined terribly as a result of the insecurity that prevailed during their administration at the coast.

- The Portuguese caused a lot of suffering to the local people as a result of their heavy taxation of the people who had already been made poor through looting and raids by the Portuguese themselves during the wars.

- There was disturbance of trade, devastation of towns and crops and burning of houses which caused untold suffering to the indigenous peoples.

- Their rule led to the depopulation of East Africa as many people lost their lives during raids as a result of the heavy punishment given to people who opposed their trade.

Revision 5

1 (a) How did the Portuguese gain control of the East African coast between 1487 and 1510?

(b) Why did the African resistance against the Portuguese fail?

2 (a) Why were the Portuguese interested in the East African coast during the 16th century?

(b)   Why had they lost their coastal empire in East Africa by 1700?

3   (a)   Why did the Portuguese lose control of the East African coast north of River Ruvuma by 1700 AD?

(b)   What were the effects of Portuguese rule on the East African coast?

4   (a)   Why did the Portuguese establish themselves on the coast of East Africa?

(b)   What were the effects of their rule on the coast?

6

The establishment of Omani power

Oman had been under Portuguese control since 1513 when Albuquerque captured Ormuz. However, early in the 17th century, the Arabs regained control of the Persian Gulf and also took control of Ormuz. Simultaneously, all the Portuguese strongholds fell to the Arabs.

It is worth noting that the Omani Arabs took a long time to reach the coast of East Africa. Around 1622, Mombasa asked for Omani aid against the Portuguese. The Imam of Oman reacted to this request by sending an expedition to ransack the Portuguese settlements in Zanzibar and Pate.

Around 1698, Fort Jesus was surrendered to the Omani invaders. The people who formed the garrison around the fort were all killed except eight Portuguese soldiers, three Indians and African women.

Zanzibar was fully occupied later and the Portuguese completely lost control over areas north of Delgado.

The expulsion of the Portuguese from the coast of East Africa however did not mean automatic establishment of Omani rule in the area. Omani rule was established a century later.

Reasons for the delay in the establishment of Omani rule at the coast

The Omanis were not interested in establishing absolute control over the coast. Instead they were content with the garrisons which they had established, with the main one being at Mombasa. There was a lot of resistance to the Omanis' establishment of their rule in East Africa. For instance, Pate invited the Portuguese back in 1727. This alliance led to the re-taking of Fort Jesus and Mombasa by the Portuguese.

The coastal people valued their independence more than everything else. They only invited the Omanis to overthrow their enemy, the Portuguese, but did not wish the Omanis to be their new rulers. So the Imam of Oman was only acknowledged but he had no real power over the coast of East Africa.

The Mazruis

The Mazruis were one of the Omani families. They came to Mombasa to serve the Yarubi Imams towards the end of the 17th century. They had taken part in the final assault on Fort Jesus and they settled in Mombasa. The Mazruis intermarried freely with the indigenous Swahili people. Later, the Mazruis became so wealthy that they began to exert a lot of influence as teachers and governors *(Walis)* of their local settlements.

Their rise to prominence started in 1727 when a member of the Mazrui family was appointed deputy governor of Mombasa. After only a few years the Mazruis reached the peak of their power at the coast. This was when the Yarubi made Mohammed ibn Uthman al-Mazrui governor of Mombasa. Shortly after this, the Yarubi were overthrown in Oman and replaced by the Busaidi. This gave the ambitious Mazruis a chance to break away from Oman and declare their independence. Other towns like Malindi, Pemba, Zanzibar, Pate and Mafia followed the example of Mombasa and declared themselves independent from Omani rule.

After this, the Mazruis set about strengthening their control both locally and further afield. They brought about peace among the different communities of Mombasa, especially among the Thalatha Taifa and Tisa Taifa, the two rivalling Swahili groups.

The Mazruis gained power through controlling the Nyika trade in the hinterland. They also seized Pemba from the Omanis and nearly took over Zanzibar. They entered into an alliance with other coastal towns like Pate, which recognised the authority of the Mazruis. However, the new Busaidi Imam did not just sit back and watch the Mazruis prosper. They engaged the Mazruis in several battles until they managed to subdue them.

The Busaidi Imams did not defeat only the Mazrui rulers of Mombasa but also the other coastal towns, commonly referred to as Mazania, which had defied them. The Omani ruler used force because he wanted to show the other towns that they could suffer the fate of Mombasa if they did not submit to him.

Because the coastal towns underestimated the powers of the Busaidi, they went to war with Oman. In a fierce battle in 1741, Mohammed bin Uthman al-Mazrui was brutally murdered and the Busaidi ruler appointed Saif bin Khalifa to govern Mombasa.

However, in 1742, Ali bin Uthman al-Mazrui, the brother of the murdered governor, overwhelmingly defeated Khalifa. This defeat induced Pate, Malindi, Mafia and Zanzibar to denounce Busaidi rule in about 1745. Unfortunately, Ali was brutally murdered by his own nephew in a battle to conquer Zanzibar. Ali's death seriously weakened Mazania and Zanzibar remained loyal to the Busaidi ruler until about 1840. Around 1780, the Omani overran Kilwa and appointed a loyal governor to rule on their behalf. However, Ahmad ibn al-Busaidi, who had been the first Busaidi, died and was replaced by his elder son, Sayyid Sultan ibn Ahmad, in about 1784.

In the same year, the brother of the new Sultan, Saifa ibn Ahmad, wanted to set up a separate sultanate on the coast of East Africa but failed. Unfortunately, Sayyid Sultan ibn Ahmad died in 1804. He was replaced by his two sons. The older Sayyid killed his brother and became an absolute ruler at the age of 15 years. Sayyid, who became known as Sayyid Said, faced a number of problems which in 1840 forced him to transfer his capital from Muscat to Zanzibar.

Reasons why Sayyid Said transferred his capital from Muscat to Zanzibar
Several factors were responsible for the transfer of Sayyid Said's capital from Muscat to Zanzibar.

- Zanzibar and the East African coast had better climatic conditions than Muscat or Oman which was very hot and had poor soil.

- Zanzibar had a deep and wide harbour where merchant ships could anchor.

- East Africa provided valuable natural resources such as ivory and gold from Sofala which Oman would want to exploit.

- Zanzibar was strategically located; therefore it could be a very good site for markets of goods from the East African mainland and other countries.

- Zanzibar had a good maritime belt which was suitable for agriculture, unlike arid Oman.

- The East African mainland was a potential source of slaves and ivory which were in very high demand the world over at that time.

- Sayyid Said wanted to promote long-distance trade at the coast and on the East African mainland.

- Sayyid Said also wanted to grow cloves on the island. At that time cloves were in high demand on the world market.

- There was very serious religious turmoil in Oman at that time, so that the only place without any religious problems was Zanzibar.

- Political persecution also necessitated the transfer of Sayyid's capital from Muscat to Zanzibar, especially after the withdrawal of the ships of the East India Company at the end of the Napoleonic wars.

- Sayyid Said's position in Oman was already insecure since there was an increase in the number of jobless robbers in the Persian Gulf.

- Sayyid Said was so ambitious that when he failed to expand his empire in Oman, he turned his attention to Zanzibar.

- The transfer of his capital from Oman to Zanzibar was also due to his earlier contact with Zanzibar and the coast of East Africa.

Revision 6

1 (a) Why did the Arabs settle on the East African coast between 1000 and 1500 AD?

   (b) What were the effects of their settlement on the coastal people?

2 (a) Why did Sayyid Said move his capital from Muscat to Zanzibar?

   (b) How did this affect Zanzibar before 1900?

7

Some interlacustrine kingdoms

The interlacustrine region refers to the area between the great lakes of East Africa. Before 1000 AD, this area was inhabited and administered by people who were not Bantu. According to oral tradition, this region was settled by the Abatembuzi, the Bachwezi and the Babito.

The interlacustrine area includes Bunyoro, Buganda, Toro, Ankole, Karagwe, Rwanda, Burundi and Wanga. Because of the soil fertility between and around the great lakes of East Africa, the Bantu, who had already settled by 1000 AD, multiplied rapidly and formed powerful kingdoms such as Bunyoro-Kitara, Buganda, Ankole, Toro and Karagwe.

Bunyoro-Kitara

Bunyoro-Kitara was one of the earliest kingdoms in East Africa. It was believed to have covered present-day Bunyoro, Toro, Ankole, Rwanda, Burundi, Buganda and Wanga. According to oral tradition, the kingdom had a line of very powerful rulers who were believed to be demi-gods. These rulers were called Abatembuzi and the traditions of the Batoro, Banyoro and Banyankore indicate that the kingdoms of Bunyoro-Kitara were founded by them.

According to the traditions of the above peoples there was a creator called Ruhinda who lived with his brother, Nkya. Nkya had four sons, Kairu, Kintu, Kahuma and Kakama. Kairu became the ancestor of all the cultivators, Kahuma that of herdsmen, and Kakama, of the rulers. Each ruler bore the title of *Omukama*.

But Kakama one time disappeared and left his son Baba to rule. Interestingly, during his reign, his people and livestock increased tremendously. According to the Bunyoro tradition,

37

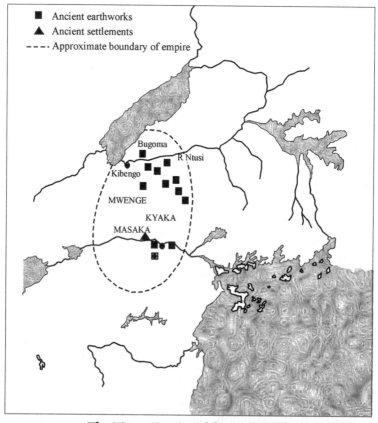

The Kitara Empire of the Bachwezi

the first death occurred during the reign of Baba. He himself died and was succeeded by Mukonko, then Ngonzaki and finally Isaza.

During the reign of Isaza, the kingdom of Kitara was divided into separate states one of which was Tsaza. Isaza married Nyamata, the daughter of Nyamiyonga, god of the underworld. Nyamata gave birth to a baby boy, Isimbwa. However, Isaza was the last king of the Abatembuzi. He also died like his predecessors and was replaced by his gatekeeper Bakuku.

The chiefs did not recognise Bakuku's supremacy and this led to the disintegration of Bunyoro-Kitara into smaller states. Bukuku was speared dead by his grandson, who was the son of Isimbwa and Nyamiru Karubumbi. Isimbwa then set about conquering all the areas that were under Bunyoro-Kitara in Ankole, Buganda, Bulega, Busoga, Toro, Madi and Bukedi. After his conquests, he changed his name to Ndahura, the first of the Chwezi kings.

The Bachwezi

The origin of the Bachwezi is still a subject of controversy. Some historians believe the Bachwezi to be of Caucasoid stock, possibly from Egypt, while others believe that the Bachwezi were Cushites who might have come from the direction of Ethiopia. The latter view is likely to hold some truth since oral tradition supports it. According to oral tradition, the Bachwezi came as strangers with their animals and imposed their rule over the people in the interlacustrine region. Like the Abatembuzi, the Bachwezi are also believed to have possessed supernatural powers.

Contributions of the Bachwezi in Bunyoro-Kitara

As new rulers of the Bunyoro-Kitara kingdom, the Bachwezi introduced a lot of changes in the kingdom:

- They introduced a centralised government or monarchy with one ruler at the apex of the administrative structure. The man at the apex was the Omukama who had powers to appoint the officials of the palace and the local government.

- The kingdom was divided into provinces with leaders appointed by the Omukama. These leaders were responsible for governing the provinces.

- The Bachwezi also introduced a standing army which they used to consolidate their rule over their subjects in Bunyoro-Kitara.

- The Bachwezi were well known for the construction of certain types of grass-thatched huts and reed houses surrounded by reed fences for the kings.

- They are remembered for the construction of ditches over 8 kilometres long around important places, for instance the ones found at Bigo Bya Mugenyi in southern Uganda. They also constructed other earthworks in Mubende and Bunyoro. All the earthworks must have been built between 1350 and 1500 AD, the approximate time of the flourishing of Chwezi culture.

- The Bachwezi are remembered for the introduction of royal regalia comprising the royal crown, drums, spears, arrows and stools.

- The Bachwezi introduced long-horned cattle in Uganda.

- They introduced the board game commonly known in Luganda as *mweso* and in Luo as *coro*.

- They introduced reed fences in the Bunyoro-Kitara kingdom.

- The cultivation of coffee is attributed to them. They are believed to have introduced coffee cultivation in Uganda.

- They introduced the art of making barkcloth and iron in the Bunyoro-Kitara kingdom.

The royal family of the Bachwezi

There are only two Bachwezi *Bakama* (kings) who are well known in the history of Bunyoro-Kitara. The two leaders are Ndahura and his son Wamara. Ndahura is said to have abdicated the throne in favour of his son Wamara and gone westwards with his wife Nyinamwiru. There they created the hot springs and crater lakes of Toro. They left permanent footmarks on a rock surface, which can still be seen today. Wamara built his capital in Bwera near the southern bank of River Katonga where he lived with his relatives.

The Bachwezi were also very fond of their cattle. This was notable especially with Mugenyi whose *Bihogo* cow was very important to him. However, after the death of Wamara, the Chwezi empire collapsed. Several reasons are believed to have precipitated the breakdown of this once prosperous empire.

Reasons for the breakdown of the Bachwezi Empire

Cattle diseases. These forced the Bachwezi to leave their empire and look for places where their animals could be safe from diseases.

Small pox. This is a contagious disease which leaves scars on the body of the victim. Small pox undermined Chwezi rule and forced the Bachwezi to abandon their empire and look for refuge in Rwanda and Karagwe.

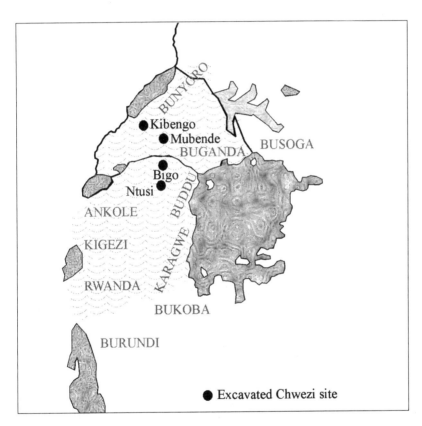

The Kitara Empire of the Bachwezi at its peak

Civil wars. The Bachwezi failed to effectively administer distant provinces because their empire was a loose one with the provincial rulers having absolute powers over their subjects. They could, therefore, easily defy the Omukama.

The death of Wamara. After Wamara's death, the subjects of the kingdom strongly resisted the rule of his successors. This discouraged the Bachwezi, leading to their downfall.

Luo invasion. What dealt the death blow to the Chwezi empire was the Luo invasion by Labongo's group which came to Bunyoro. The Luo invasion sent the Bachwezi fleeing in disarray. Tradition has it that they moved southwards.

The Babito dynasty

It was the Luo who founded the Babito dynasty in Bunyoro. These Luo were part of the Luo migration of the River Lake Nilotes who migrated from Sudan to Pubungo, then on to Bunyoro. They found the Bachwezi kingdom crumbling and they took advantage of that weakness to establish themselves as rulers in Bunyoro. The founder of the Babito dynasty was a man called Rukidi Mpuga who sometimes is believed to be Labongo. He became the first Mubito king in Bunyoro.

However, when the Luo took over the administration of Bunyoro they found that the culture of the Bachwezi was superior to theirs and Rukidi Mpuga had to learn to respect Chwezi culture. What the Babito copied from Chwezi culture included palace architecture and royal drums, notably two, known as *Kajumba* and *Nyalebo*. But the Babito also contributed immensely to the enrichment of Nyoro culture. For instance, they introduced pet names or *empako* such as Amooti and Akiiki. The pet name *Okali* was reserved strictly for the Omukama (king).

In addition, the Babito introduced new items of regalia which included the throne (*Nya myawo*), royal drums known as *Tibamulinda* and *Nyakangubi*, a spear, a shield, a horn, sandals, a rake, a royal fire and a bag of millet.

The Babito further established the system of granting land to clans. This was the origin of the Bataka system in which each clan became the landowner of specific areas of the kingdom. This system was maintained by their children in Buganda. Furthermore, they also introduced the practice of royal burial, involving separate burial sites for jawbones and bodies of *Abakama* (Kings). All these practices led to the development of shrines whose sites can still be seen in Bunyoro.

The organisation of Bunyoro Kingdom
All the chiefs or rulers of Bunyoro belonged to the royal clan of Babito. The non-Babito were excluded from administration. The Omukama was responsible for posting those rulers to various provinces or *saza* into which the kingdom was divided. It has been said that all those provinces formed a federation which was loosely governed by the Omukama.

Owing to the size of the kingdom, those provinces were actually semi-independent. The saza chiefs were allowed to raise their own provincial armies called *obwesengeze*. However, some very strong and talented Abakama were able to unite the kingdom. Such men included Omukama Kabalega. The Omukama had no standing army to keep law and order. This resulted in some provinces breaking away and becoming independent. During the reigns of three kings – Olimi 1, Nyabongo 1 and Owinyi – Bunyoro lost Ankole, Karagwe, Rwanda and Busoga. During the reign of Duhaga 1, Bunyoro lost Kooki and around 1830, Bunyoro lost Toro.

Reasons for the decline of Bunyoro-Kitara
When the kingdom of Bunyoro reached the peak of its greatness, it started to decline and finally collapsed. It became a small kingdom whose glory was revived by great men like Kamurasi and Kabalega until their efforts were brought to an end by the British. There were various reasons for the drastic decline and eventual collapse of the kingdom:

- The empire was so vast that it was impossible for the Omukama to effectively control it.

- Poor communication between the Omukama and his chiefs complicated the administration of the kingdom, with the chiefs largely being left to their own devices.

- The rulers of the Babito were very discriminatory, with only people from the Babito house being allowed to rule.

- The Babito rulers were cattle keepers who exploited and oppressed the agriculturalists. This complicated the relationship between the Babito and the non-Babito.

- The chiefs and their subjects sometimes rebelled against the Omukama and broke away from his administration.

- Babito rule was also characterised by a series of succession wars. There was no clear-cut law on succession, such that when the Omukama died wars usually ensued over his jawbones, for whoever took possession of them was entitled to the throne. These wars caused a lot of losses and devastation as well as famine. This not only weakened the population but also reduced the number of people in the Kingdom.

Another big blow to the Nyoro empire was the emergence of the Buganda kingdom in the 18th and 19th centuries. Bunyoro lost Busoga, Kyaggwe, Bugerere and Bulemezi to Buganda. During the reign of Jjunju, the Kabaka of Buganda, Bunyoro was conquered and Buddu (the present Masaka district) was annexed by Buganda.

The breaking away of Buganda from Bunyoro was disastrous for Bunyoro. Later the Baganda even supported the British to conquer Bunyoro. The British conquest of Bunyoro represented the death blow to the once famous kingdom in the interlacustrine region.

Karagwe Empire

The land of Karagwe was occupied by the Bantu who followed the south-west route into East Africa between the 5th and 10th centuries. After about two or three generations, these people moved north-eastwards. Their movement started again between the 9th and 10th centuries, northwards into Ankole, especially around Buhweju near Ibanda in Mbarara district. Meanwhile, others continued to Toro and Bunyoro.

During the 10th century, the Karagweans went back to Karagwe, most of them having intermingled with the pastoralists from Bunyoro-Kitara. The first Bantu people to settle in Karagwe before the Chwezi people migrated there were the Banyambo.

Economic organisation

The people of Karagwe practised agriculture. They grew crops such as sorghum, yam and millet. The land was very fertile and as such agriculture became the backbone of their economy. Karagwe also enjoyed reliable rainfall. The people of Karagwe also kept livestock. In fact, most of them were pastoralists. They also practised fishing, especially in the south-western part of Lake Victoria and on rivers such as the Kagera.

Later, the people of Karagwe got involved in long-distance trade, when it was introduced by the Arabs. The trade route from the coast via Nyamwezi to Buganda cut through Karagwe. The Arabs bartered goods such as beads, chinaware and iron coils for local trade items such as ivory.

Political organisation

Like in any other kingdom within the interlacustrine region, the clan was the basic political unit in Karagwe. There were many clans and all these were composed of many different families. There were also many sub-clans or lineages. Later, though, the clans were integrated into larger political systems which were amalgamated into a large kingdom headed by the dominant Sita tribe. The last ruler of this clan (Sita) was Nono.

During the reign of Nono, i.e. around the 16th century, Ruhinda led his Chwezi immigrants from the north into Karagwe. He had left Ankole with his followers and moved into present-day Bukoba district in Tanzania. Nono was deposed by Ruhinda and a new dynasty called Hinda was founded. Later he sent out his sons, each with a royal drum, to establish Hinda sub-dynasties in Gisaka, Kyamtwara, Ihangiro, Buzinza, Busubi, Ukerewe and Nana. All these principalities came under the Hinda dynasty.

The clan and sub-clan organisations continued to exist at the local level with each clan having a head and an elder known as *Muharaambwa* in charge of religious rites. All these clans were grouped under the principalities founded by the sons of Ruhinda and as such they were administered by various chiefs.

The chiefdoms were Kianja, Bukara, Kyamtwara, Kiziba, Bugabo, Misenyi and Karagwe. The clan heads were responsible for the collection and payment of tributes to the chiefs. The chiefs had the power to dismiss their clan heads if their people complained about them.

Each chiefdom called itself *Ihanga*, which means 'the nation'. The chief was a supreme judge who had powers of life and death over his subjects. The chief also had powers over land. He could grant land or take it away it from anyone within his dominion. He had, however, to always allocate land according to customary law. Thus, the authority of the chief was not left unchecked. If he proved to be highly dictatorial, his people either dismissed him or migrated from his dominion to a rival chiefdom.

Social organisation

Among the reforms brought about in Karagwe by the Chwezi was the age-set system by which boys of the same age lived together at the local chief's residence. These boys were trained in many ways: some received military training, others were trained in court manners; they were also taught good manners. Their culture was closely connected with long-horned cattle, which were a symbol of wealth.

The religious beliefs of the Bahinda were also introduced. They believed in a supreme god and the spirits of their ancestors. They had some royal regalia, for instance drums which were very important in their tradition. Evil spirits were exorcised through offerings and sacrifices.

Reasons for the collapse of Karagwe

- The invasion of the empire by the Banyoro in the 1770s during the reign of Ntare VI. This led to the destruction of the once vast empire.

- Internal conflicts as the various states created by the sons of Ruhinda rivalled one another and struggled for their own independence.

- The death of Ruhinda, since after his death there was nobody who could unite the people.

Nkore

This kingdom was probably established by Ruhinda and his clan after their independence from the Bachwezi. The Bahinda clan moved from the south-west into western Uganda around 1350 AD. A new dynasty, with Ruhinda as its first ruler, settled in Isingiro which was the headquarters of the kingdom. The kingdom was ruled by the *Omugabe*.

The ruling clan in Nkore claimed to be the descendants of the Bachwezi who were regarded as gods. Ruhinda, their leader, was believed to be the son of a slave girl who was married by a Muchwezi in Mbarara, the Nkore capital.

At first, Ankole was a very weak kingdom. For instance, at the beginning of the 18th century, Omukama Gwamali of Bunyoro invaded it, but he was killed in Rwanda and his retreating soldiers were killed in Nkore by Omugabe Ntare. But Nkore became very powerful during the reign of Ntare IV who extended the boundaries of Nkore to include River Katonga, as well as the counties of Sheema and Rwampara which had been part of Mpororo. In the mid 18th century, Omugabe Rwebishengye seized the pasture land of Kabula from Bunyoro. Omugabe Mutambuka conquered Igara and Buhweju in the 19th century. He also raided Toro, Busongora and Karagwe. His successor was Ntare V who signed a treaty with Lugard, thus putting Nkore under British rule.

Political organisation

Politically, the Omugabe was the head of the kingdom. In theory, his decisions were final. The Abagabe were frequently competent people who ruled with great skill and ability. Just below the king was the *Enganzi* (prime minister) who assisted the Omugabe in ruling the kingdom. The kingdom was divided into sixteen districts, with each of them ruled by a *Mukungu* appointed by the Omugabe.

The *Abakungu* (plural of *Mukungu)* were supposed to keep law and order and also to be responsible for feeding the Omugabe and the people in his palace. They were therefore expected to regularly send beer and millet to the palace. The army commanders were appointed by the Omugabe himself on the advice of the royal diviners.

Economic organisation

The Nkore people were divided into two distinct social classes, which had a significant effect on their economic organisation. There was a cattle owning class (Bahima) and the cultivators (Bairu). The Bahima produced milk, meat, hides, while the Bairu provided grains, yams and iron goods. The Bahima who had close social links with the Bahinda rulers, moved from place to place in search of water and pasture. The Bairu lived in permanent clan-based villages. The main food crops grown by the cultivators were millet and legumes.

The blacksmiths were from among the Bairu, and they made hoes, knives, etc. The peasants also undertook other economic activities such as pottery and carpentry. They made pots, stools, wooden dishes, etc. Owning cattle was prestigious.

Social organisation

As already stated, socially the people of Nkore – or the Banyankore – were divided into two classes, i.e. the Bahima and the Bairu. The Bahinda, part of the Bahima, were the rulers while the Bairu were the serfs. In fact, a Muiru was supposed to obey any Muhima without question.

There was a royal drum called *Bagyendanwa* which was respected by all Banyankore. In every family, there was a shrine at which milk, beer and all other foodstuffs would be offered to the spirits of the dead. The Banyankore also believed in a supreme God, Ruhanga. He was believed to be the creator.

Revision 7

1 (a) Who were the Bachwezi?

   (b) Account for their contribution to the history of East Africa.

2 (a) Why did the Chwezi empire disintegrate?

   (b) Explain the origin of Batembuzi.

3 (a) How did Ruhinda establish his control over Karagwe?

(b) What changes did he introduce?

4 (a) What were the contributions of the Babito in the history of Bunyoro-Kitara?

(b) Describe the social, political and economic organisation of the Banyankore.

5. Explain the importance of the following in the history of Uganda:

(a) Batembuzi (Tembuzi).

(b) Bachwezi (Chwezi).

(c) What were the origins of the Chwezi (Bachwezi)?

(d) Explain the importance of the Bachwezi in the history of East Africa.

6. Describe the contribution of the Bachwezi in the histry of Bunyoro-Kitara:

(a) How did Ruhinda establish his control over Karagwe?

(b) What changes did he introduce?

7. Describe the contribution of the following people in the histroy of Bunyoro-Kitara:

(a) Bachwezi

(b) Babito

8. Describe the social, political and economic organisation of the Banyankore.

8

Buganda

The first published book on the history of Buganda was written by Sir Apollo Kagwa. It is entitled *Basekabaka ba Buganda (The Kings of Buganda)* and was published in 1901.

Origin

The Baganda were one of the Bantu clans which had been living within their present homeland since 1000 AD. Some clans joined them later. These clans claimed to have come with Kintu. Kintu was the founder of the Buganda kingdom. He came from the eastern direction, probably from the Mt Elgon area. However, some clans claim that they came to Buganda with Kato Kimera who, according to Bunyoro-Kitara tradition, was a brother to Isingoma Rukidi Mpuga. Although some historians (especially Baganda historians) disagree that Kimera came from Bunyoro-Kitara, Kimera might have come to Buganda from the north as a result of the Luo invasion.

The growth of Buganda

The Buganda kingdom started from a very small area called Kyadondo. Around the 14th and 15th centuries it expanded from Kyadondo to include Busiro and Busujju.

In the 15th century, Buganda was still a very insignificant state under the control of a king called *Kabaka*. The Kabaka's authority at that time was limited by the powers of the clan heads called *Bataka*. At that time the Kabaka was more of an arbitrator than a ruler. The constant raids on Buganda created an urgent need for unity. The raids were always from Bunyoro. The survival of the Baganda, therefore, depended on their unity.

The Kabaka and his court began to be seen as the centre of both political and military authority. From the 18th century

50

onwards, Buganda expanded rapidly. For instance, during the reign of Jjunju, Buddu and Bwera were annexed. Later, in the first year of the 19th century, Buwekula was also conquered. Further expansion of the Buganda kingdom was helped by the weakness of the Bunyoro kingdom. As Bunyoro declined, Buganda occupied the bordering lands such as Ssingo, Bulemezi, Buruli and Bugerere.

Factors responsible for the rise and expansion of Buganda kingdom

Several factors were responsible for the rise and growth of the Buganda kingdom, among which was her strategic position. The land is near Lake Victoria, which made it easy to acquire fish for food and for the people to have access to water transport, which made the kingdom prosper. It was also small and compact, with Lake Victoria providing security from external attack on its southern boundary. Furthermore, the land was well watered and this made agriculture and permanent settlement easy. This therefore made its population grow rapidly.

As a result of its location around the lake, food crops like bananas and vegetables could be grown throughout the year because rainfall was regular and reliable. Because of the abundance of food, Buganda's population grew rapidly and this created pressures for the expansion of the once very small kingdom. In fact, by the 19th century the population of Buganda had reached half a million people.

Permanent settlements which had been promoted by the practice of agriculture also made centralised administration very easy to carry out, hence facilitating the growth of the Buganda kingdom into the most powerful state in the 19th century. The administration, centred around the Kabaka, made it easy to mobilise the Baganda to conquer other states, hence enlarging the kingdom.

Another important factor was the weakness of other states such as Bunyoro. For instance, the Baganda were able to capture Buddu and Bwera because the authority of the Omukama of Bunyoro had been weakened.

The traditions of the Baganda also helped in the rise and growth of the kingdom. For instance, the Baganda regarded the Kabaka as a demi-god whose word had to be obeyed and every wish satisfied. The Buganda kings therefore took advantage of the loyalty of their subjects to expand their kingdom.

Another factor which favoured the rise and rapid growth of Buganda was external influence, especially from the Arabs and Europeans in the 19th century. Buganda gained prominence as a result of acquiring guns from these external forces. These guns were used in the immediate expansion of the kingdom.

Political organisation

The Kabaka was the head of the kingdom. He was regarded as a semi-divine being whose word was not questioned. The Kabaka appointed his administrative officials to help him. They had their particular duties to execute in the kingdom.

Among the top officials appointed by the Kabaka was the *Katikkiro* (prime minister), *Omulamuzi* (the chief justice) and *Omuwanika* (the treasurer).

The kingdom was also divided into counties, sub-counties and parishes with chiefs being appointed by the Kabaka to govern on his behalf.

There was also a court or *Lukiiko* which was the centre of administration. Each clan was expected to send their sons to the court to be educated and given jobs. These people were called pages or *Bagalagala*. Promotion at the court was through military or civil service to the Kabaka. The Kabaka's power to appoint chiefs weakened the Bataka (clan leaders) who had been a hindrance to the unity of the kingdom.

Social organisation

The Baganda believed that the spirits of the dead had an influence in the day-to-day affairs of the living. They believed that such spirits caused trouble for their relatives. Such spirits were called *balubaale* and were always consulted through spirit mediums and prophets. Different balubaale had different responsibilities. For instance, Dungu was consulted for hunting, Musoke for rain, Nagawonyi in case of drought.

There were also traditional healers called *basawo abaganda* who used herbs to cure. In Ganda society, the Kabaka was referred to as *Ssabasajja* – 'first among men' – or *Ssabataka* – 'first among clan heads'. Ganda society was also divided into many social classes. For instance, there were common men called *bakopi*; there were also the *abami* or rulers, who included the *batongole* or chiefs. There were, however, opportunities for upward mobility from a *mukopi* (singular of *bakopi*) to a ruler or a chief depending on one's ability.

The Kabaka married from all the clans to ensure unity among the Baganda. There was no particular clan which was considered to be superior to the other clans. Any clan was capable of producing a Kabaka. The Kabaka belonged to his mother's clan.

All the dead kings were buried in a royal tomb. Also all the Baganda clans had their burial grounds where they buried their dead relatives.

The Baganda also preserved the jawbones of their ancestors. The jawbones of their prominent men were kept in memory of their work. The drums, spears and royal shield were kept in the royal courts.

Economic organisation

Goats and cattle were kept by the Kabaka and his men for food. The Baganda practised agriculture. Women looked after the gardens while the men were always busy fighting. Crops included bananas, coffee, vegetables and, later in the 19th century, cotton. All land in Buganda belonged to the Kabaka. He appointed his headmen who were responsible for the distribution of land to the peasants in the society.

Later on, around 1844, the Baganda got involved in trade. This brought a lot of prosperity to the kingdom. In fact, with the coming of the Arabs and Europeans, trade became very important.

The Baganda also manufactured barkcloth. This was very important as it brought a lot of wealth to the Baganda as other tribes such as Banyoro and Basoga bought the cloth from them. Among other enterprises which the Baganda got involved in was ironworking. Some iron implements were manufactured by the Baganda themselves.

The manufacture of canoes was another important economic activity since most of the Baganda lived near the lake. The canoes were used for fishing and water transport. They were not meant for transporting goods only, but also warriors to wage war.

By the second half of the 19th century, the Buganda kingdom had become very powerful in trade within East Africa. Trade was conducted between Buganda and Arabs and also with Swahili traders. Baganda supplied the Arabs and Swahili with ivory, slaves and other goods in exchange for guns and gunpowder, cloth, beads and glassware.

Military organisation

All able-bodied men in Buganda were supposed to participate in military activities to defend Buganda. Men always went to war while women remained at home to carry on with agricultural work. With the introduction of canoes, the military strength of the Buganda army increased as they could travel faster to attack and subdue their enemies. The Kabaka was the commander-in-chief of his armed forces.

Revision 8

1 (a) What factors led to Buganda's strength in the 18th and 19th centuries?

   (b) Describe Buganda's relations with its neighbours.

2 (a) Describe the political, social and economic organisation of the Baganda before 1850.

3 (a) Describe the origins of the Kingdom of Buganda.

   (b) What factors led to its expansion up to 1850?

4 (a) Describe the rise and expansion of the Kingdom of Buganda up to 1850.

   (b) Why did it become powerful during this period?

9

Other East African peoples

The Nyamwezi

The Nyamwezi were among the early Bantu immigrants into Tanzania. They occupied the central part of Tanzania especially the area around present-day Tabora. They were called Nyamwezi, meaning 'people of the moon' because they came from the west, the direction from which the new moon rises.

The Nyamwezi had different origins and they did not exist as a united society by the 18th century. Even when they settled at Unyamwezi, which is the central plateau around Tabora, they lived in numerous small self-governing groups without any single central political authority. Originally, the Nyamwezi were agriculturalists and fishermen who supplemented their livelihood by raising cattle. Later, the Nyamwezi became prominent pioneers of long-distance trade in eastern and central Africa.

Organisation of Ntemi chiefdom

Though the Nyamwezi were not united under any one political organisation, they organised themselves into smaller political units, referred to as *Ntemi,* based on kinship ties or belief in common origins. Among the Ntemi associations were the Unyongilwa, Usagali, Ussongo, Usumba and Usiha, each of which had its own chief. These chiefs were the officials at the centre of affairs. They obtained their orders directly from the Ntemi chief.

The influence of the Ntemi chief did not extend very far from his headquarters. He therefore always relied on the *Gunguli*, the heads of the various settlement areas. The Gunguli in turn relied on the *Wazanga Makaya* or heads of households.

It must, however, be emphasised that the Ntemi chiefs were not despotic; they exercised true democracy by sharing powers with those under their jurisdiction.

The functions of the Ntemi chiefs were political, religious and judicial. They had the authority to declare war on the advice of their council; also before they could make peace, they had to consult the council. The chiefs were also the overall controllers of land. They made sure that it was properly utilised and that food stocks were constantly replenished. They also supplied those struck by disaster as well as the needy among their followers, with food from their stores.

Furthermore, their judicial duties included the settling of disputes among their people and the hearing of cases of murder, treason and witchcraft. They administered justice according to their customary laws. The chiefs were the intermediaries between their people and their ancestors. They were the only people who could perform certain ceremonies and sacrifices.

The general health of the Ntemi chiefs depended on the happiness of their society. Eventually the post of Ntemi chief became hereditary.

The Nandi (1500 - 1800)

The Nandi people are part of the Plains Nilotes who emerged as a force in East Africa in about 1000 AD. The Nandi were a small group who lived along the escarpment that separate the present-day Nandi district from Nyanza. During the 17th century, the Nandi moved northwards until they came face to face with another group, the Maasai of the Uasin Gishu plateau. The Nandi people had semi-independent units of administration called *bororpisiek*, each controlled by a council of elders called *kok*. The council of elders who controlled the bororpisiek were chosen for their wisdom and military skills. They frequently met to discuss the affairs of state over beer. Their decisions were then conveyed to other groups, including the young warriors.

However, at this stage, there was no central authority to control the whole of Nandi land, but in times of emergency, or of war, a territorial council would be formed of representatives from the various bororpisiek called *koburetap pororiet.*

What always threatened the peace of the Nandi people was the presence of the Maasai to the north of their country. There were therefore several clashes between the Nandi and the Maasai warriors.

By the early 19th century, the threat from the Maasai warriors had begun to decline and the Nandi became quite powerful. During the last thirty years of that century, the Nandi became the most powerful people in western Kenya. They went raiding in small units in order to capture cattle. Their raids were not intended to capture territory. In the 1870s, after the Maasai civil wars, the Nandi defeated the Kwavi and the Purko, and by the 1880s they were raiding all their neighbours except the Kipsigis.

The Nandi clan units were divided into age-sets. Their men were initiated during adolescence and formed closely-knit age-sets. Their initiation occurred at five-year intervals. A number of these age-sets formed an age-group.

The age-set system strengthened the military might of the Nandi as the junior age-sets formed the armed wing of their military. The age-sets also had a section of *kiriogik* (lawyers) who advised the kok (elders) on how to settle disputes among the Nandi people.

Originally, the Nandi were hunters and they used dogs and traps as well as spears, bows and arrows. They used very sophisticated hunting and trapping methods. But later they started keeping animals like cattle, goats and sheep for meat. Cattle also provided milk and blood which was extracted from the jugular vein by means of a thin, sharp arrow. Women's work was to milk the cows. Cultivation was also important and the Nandi grew vegetables.

Later, after the decline of the Maasai, the Nandi inherited an element of the Maasai culture, the *orkoiyot.* This became evident when a member of Oloiboni, a Maasai family noted for its great prophetic qualities, moved and settled in Nandi land. His name was Barsabotwo. His advice soon made the

Nandi people victorious in many wars against the Luo. His authority therefore increased tremendously and he became a consultant to the bororpisiek on sensitive issues.

However, Barsabotwo died in 1860 and his children fought over his throne but none of them succeeded in taking it. In the 1880s his grandson emerged victorious. He was called Kimnyolei. He predicted, among other things, the coming of the white men who would conquer Nandi land and a snake, spitting fire and smoke, which would run along the escarpment - reference to the Uganda Railway. The Nandi therefore became very powerful once they were unified by orkoiyot. They constantly harassed their neighbours but were only checked in the 19th century by the British.

The Maasai

Origin

The Maasai people are part of the Plains Nilotes whose main dispersal area is believed to have been around the Lake Rudolf area. By the second millenium, i.e. from about 1000 AD, the Plains Nilotes emerged as a force to reckon with in East Africa.

From the Lake Rudolf area, it is believed that one of the Maasai groups, the Bari-speakers, moved into Sudan, leaving another group behind which later split into three: the Lutuko, the Karimojong - Teso and the Maasai. Among the second group however, the Maasai became the most prominent. The Lutuko settled in Sudan, the Karimojong - Teso moved towards Mount Elgon, while the Maasai moved south-east towards Mount Kenya and then throughout most parts of central Kenya and northern Tanzania. Being pastoralists, they settled in the area between Mt Kenya and Mt Kilimanjaro, and also around the Taita hills. Here they lived among the Chagga and the Kikuyu. During the 17th century the Maasai moved into the Uasin-Gishu plateau and by 1800, they had spread far to the south, into what is now Tanzania.

Social organisation

The Maasai split up into about sixteen independent groups. Each of those groups had its own territory, water supply and grazing land. They were organised into clans which were divided into age-sets. These age-sets had different names and also different cattle brands. Initiation into an age-set was through circumcision at roughly fifteen-year intervals.

After circumcision, the young initiates joined the grade of junior warriors, locally called *Ilmurran*. This happened about seven years after circumcision. After about seven years of being warriors, they would be promoted to junior elders, and after another period of about fifteen years they would become senior elders.

Administration and leadership were exercised through the system of age-sets. At the head of every age-set was an *Olaiguanami* whose task was always to plan any military attacks by the warriors in his age-set. He was also responsible for the distribution of any booty from the war, for instance women, children or cattle, to his army men. Each of the sixteen groups had at its head a ritual leader called *Laibon*. His duty was more religious than political.

Court cases were always presided over by the elders in their society. In case someone was found guilty of committing an offence which he had been accused of, he was ordered to pay a fine of cattle. If the case was murder, it was treated differently. The accused, if found guilty, had to pay a fine of 49 head of cattle to the clan of the victim. Sometimes, however, the clan of the victim would avenge by killing one member from the clan of the murderer.

The Maasai had some kind of class system. They had the blacksmith class. This class of people were considered inferior and their importance was based solely on their skills in the manufacture of spears, shields and swords. The blacksmiths had no legal rights or even the means of revenge if a Maasai killed one of their numbers. But if the other ones killed a Maasai, the Maasai would avenge by killing many blacksmiths.

Economically, animal husbandry was the most important activity among the Maasai people. Cattle were kept for their milk, blood, skins and hides. The Maasai also kept sheep and donkeys. The Maasai obtained vegetables and grains from their neighbours, the Kikuyu in exchange for soda, skins, beans and cowrie shells. They established markets where they could meet and exchange their goods. For instance, the Maasai exchanged hides and butter for beans, millet, tobacco, red ochre and sugar cane.

The Maasai brewed their drinks locally from Okiek honey. Although they had access to fish, the Maasai considered eating it a taboo. The main activity of the males among the Maasai was to herd cattle, while the females were responsible for milking the cows and bartering of their goods at markets.

On religion, the Maasai had their supreme God, *Enkai*, who was believed to have the power of life and death. Prayers were offered to Enkai through the *Laibon* who was believed to have been endowed by the Enkai with magical and religious powers. The Laibon prayed for rain, and also cured sickness. It was also his responsibility to make charms for the warriors in order to protect them during the wars. The prayers to Enkai were always offered under the sacred trees which acted as shrines.

Maasai cattle raid

The Kwavi

The Maasai are believed to have moved southwards into an area which had been under the control of the Kalenjin in about 1700AD. They subsequently absorbed much of the Kalenjin culture, including many Kalenjin words. They took control of the area and became prominent administrators.

By 1800, the Maasai had become very powerful in central Kenya and northern Tanzania. They roamed vast areas of land which they used for grazing their animals, but they had no control over that land.

The Maasai and the Kwavi were related. They spoke similar languages and their customs were similar. The Kwavi include the Samburu, Laikipiak, I Kinapop, Uasin-Gishu, Lasegelei and the Kapenabisi. All these were more powerful than the pastoral Maasai.

By the 19th century, the Maasai had become prominent in East Africa as a fierce people who usually went on the rampage, raiding their neighbours. The raids were usually carried out in order to replenish or increase their animal herds and they always occurred during the dry season.

The Maasai were disciplined warriors who spent several years in military training. A successful cattle raid earned the raiders social prestige. It must be noted that the Kwavi were initially pastoralists but they were forced to become agriculturalists in the 19th century. The wars between the Kwavi and Maasai seemed to have started in about 1815 on the Uasin-Gishu plateau. The civil wars between the two ethnic groups started as a result of the growth in the population of the two groups. As their populations grew, there was no land for expansion and as such rivalry over limited grazing land triggered the wars. Very many wars were fought in the 1840s when the Kwavi of Laikipia, who enjoyed support from Maasai living south of Lake Naivasha, defeated the Kwavi of Uasin-Gishu.

The civil wars in Maasailand continued into the second half of the 19th century. All these wars weakened the Maasai as a military community. Later, the defeated Uasin-Gishu fought the Purko, driving them out of the Rift Valley. But the Purko soon counterattacked the Kwavi and defeated them. The Kwavi were almost wiped out from the Uasin-Gishu plateau; the few who survived took refuge among the Chagga, Kikuyu, the people around Taveta, Arusha and the Kenyan coast.

Between 1870 and 1875, the Laikipia Kwavi were also defeated by their former allies, the Purko and their neighbours. The numerous civil wars weakened the Kwavi as a military community. The Kwavi had been powerful but when they attacked the pastoral Maasai, they suffered terrible defeat. Many homes were also devastated as a result of the wars; and many people had to flee their homes and look for asylum in other areas. The wars led to the death of many Kwavi and Maasai, hence their depopulation.

Reasons for Maasai dominance over the people of East Africa between 17th and 19th centuries:

- The Maasai were very able warriors. With their long spears, shields of hide, clubs, war-paint and ostrich feather plumes, the sight of the Maasai warriors alone was enough to frighten their enemies into submission.

- The Maasai people were very courageous.

- The Maasai, time and again, fought as allies with rulers of Wanga and Chief Rindi of the Chagga, thus gaining prominence and influence.

- The Maasai were not only brave warriors, but they also controlled a number of important caravan routes. Because of their control of such trade routes, all travellers wishing to cross their territory had to pay for that privilege.

- The Maasai people established cordial relations with their neighbours such as the Kikuyu and the Chagga by encouraging inter-marriages and trade. Trade routes which the Kikuyu called *Njira Cia Agendi* were open even in times of war.

However, Maasai influence did not last beyond the 19th century. Their influence seriously declined during the 19th century for the following reasons:

- Their own civil wars, which became very frequent in the 19th century. All these civil wars led to the disintegration of their solidarity as some Maasai took refuge among their neighbours, the Kikuyu.

- The Maasai and the Kwavi were struck by natural calamities like small pox, cholera and rinderpest which killed almost all their large herds of cattle as well as people.

- Famine became widespread and left them helpless. Their decline facilitated the rise of the Nandi people.

- Locusts also destroyed their pastures, leaving their animals to starve to death.

- The Maasai were conservative, therefore they stuck to their traditions. Otherwise they could have embraced Arab and European ways of living.

- Another serious problem was the succession dispute after the death of Laibon Supet.

The Chagga

The Chagga people are part of the Eastern Bantu. Their present homeland is around the southern slopes of Mt. Kilimanjaro in Tanzania. This area is very fertile. Because of this the Chagga people got attracted to this land. In addition to its fertility, it also has a very good climate and reliable rainfall.

The main economic activity of the Chagga was agriculture. Their agricultural methods were quite advanced. They practised crop rotation and also applied animal manure in their gardens. They also used irrigation. The banana was their staple food crop. Besides bananas, the Chagga also grew coffee and eleusine. They always made sure that they grew surplus food for trade. In fact, food items were bartered for cattle and ironware. The Chagga also kept cattle and goats, from which they obtained milk, hides and skins which they used for the payment of bride wealth. They even practised zero-grazing. Women would fetch grass for the cattle to eat.

Among the Chagga, possession of a very large herd of cattle was a source of greatness and prestige. One's wealth was estimated in accordance with the number of cattle one had. In addition to zero-grazing, the Chagga always grazed their animals on the slopes of Mount Kilimanjaro.

Trade was very important among the Chagga people. Many of their chiefs participated in it. For instance, Chief Rombo encouraged trade with the Arabs at the coast. Trade with the Swahili flourished during the time of Chief Rindi.

Chagga society was organised such that it had a hierarchy of officials with a chief at the apex of the administrative structure. The chiefs had judicial and religious powers over their people. All important cases were solved by the chiefs. Security was of paramount importance to the Chagga people, therefore the chief had control over it. His main responsibility was to see to it that there was peace throughout his dominion.

There were also other people who would help a chief in his administrative roles. Second to him was an administrator who was expected to take orders from him. Sometimes, in the absence of a Chagga chief, such a person would preside over any court.

There was also a group of people, usually elders, who advised the chief. They were very influential in matters of governance. They were heads of the local clans, their main role being mainly of a judicial nature. Their taxes or tributes were collected by the village headmen and remitted to the chief of the area. These tributes were usually in the form of finger millet.

Socially, the Chagga people were well organised; they worshipped one God called *Ruwa*. Ruwa was the name of the sun as well. He was believed to have liberated mankind by providing him with fruits and good edible plants. The Chagga also adored the spirits of the dead, giving them offerings. The ritual of kinship was very important to them.

The Kikuyu

The early history of the Kikuyu is not well known, but their ancestors are believed to have migrated from Meru, particularly from the areas currently occupied by the Tharaka and Igembe.

One of the Kikuyu legends refers to Mukurwe wa Gathanga as the place where God or Ngai appeared and created their ancestor, Gikuyu, and his wife Mumbi. However, another legend holds that a certain Mbere man had four sons who respectively became the ancestors of the Kikuyu, the Kamba, the Athi and Maasai peoples.

By the 16th century the early Kikuyu had settled in Mbere and Chuka. Later, due to population pressure and external forces, mainly represented by the Galla people, the Kikuyu were forced to move to the Mwea plains where they settled around Ithanga.

During the first half of the 18th century, the Kikuyu moved to Othanga and Oguthi in Nyeri, Tetu, Mathira, Kiambu and Nyandina. All these movements were due to population pressure.

During the 19th century they expanded into those areas. They encountered opposition only from the Maasai. Other groups which they met included the Athi and the Gumba. The Kikuyu adopted some aspects of the culture of the Athi people, for instance circumcision of males and clitoridectomy (cutting off of the women's clitorises). They also adopted the age-set system.

Social structure

The Kikuyu people, like their neighbours the Maasai, were also organised into clans. There were about nine clans which were named according to the nine daughters of their legendary father, Gikuyu. Every clan was made up of age-sets. Each of the age-sets had a name which often marked a particular event. In order to join an age-set, one had to be initiated. This was done through circumcision which always took place when the one was eighteen years of age. The initiation took place at intervals of five to nine years. In the next four years no initiation took place. Each of these groups constituted a fighting force. Women were initiated every year, and they either came up with their own names or they adopted the name of their age-set.

The soldiers elected a leader who was their spokesman in the council of elders. Political offices were held by an age-set for a certain period of time. Once that time was over, that age-set retired only to be replaced by a younger age-set. Junior warriors had the task of clearing the land, guarding the villages from wild animals, constructing cattle pens, clearing paths and doing all other activities assigned to them by the elders. The senior warriors were allowed to marry, after becoming junior elders. Sometimes the senior warriors were allowed to become junior elders after giving a goat and a calabash of beer.

After the circumcision of a man's first born, he paid two more goats and beer before becoming a senior elder. After making such a payment, he was accepted in the *ki ama* (council of elders).

The kiama was responsible for the making and passing of laws. Their big task was also to ensure justice, which was enforced by the soldiers. Members of the kiama were the only people who, as a group, offered prayers to Ngai. The kiama settled disputes, and imposed fines on the accused if he or she was found guilty.

The Kikuyu were predominantly agriculturalists who grew cereals like sorghum, maize and eleusine. They also grew beans, cow peas, lima beans, pigeon peas, bananas, sugar cane, taro and yams. The Kikuyu exchanged their crops in the markets for Maasai goods.

Markets were very important to the Kikuyu people. They were found in almost all villages, with the oldest ones being at Giitwa, Karatina, Gacatha, Gakindu and Muthithi. In these markets, pottery, baskets and many other goods, including farm produce, were sold. Markets were held every fourth day of the week.

Coffee was also grown as a major cash crop during the colonial era. Land was very important to the Kikuyu; no man would marry without land. The Kikuyu also kept cattle, goats and bees for honey. Milk and ghee were obtained from the cattle and goats. They did not engage in fishing and neither did they keep chickens since it was taboo for them to eat fish and birds. Men demarcated their land by planting lilies and trees around its perimeter. Women cultivated, sowed and harvested the crops. The Kikuyu believed that Ngai had powers over the sun, moon, stars, rainbow, thunder and lightning. The presence of all those manifested the presence of Ngai.

Ngai was only to be approached by the elders as a community but not by individuals.

Ngai lived on Mount Kenya, which is known by the local Kikuyu as Kirinyaga. Shrines were built around Kirinyaga in order to worship Ngai. Witches and evil spirits were believed to be the cause of misfortune and epidemics. Spirits were driven away by blowing horns, beating drums, etc.

As we have already seen, the Kikuyu were divided into clans. Each family had a head and above the head of the family was a *mbari*. Mbari in fact was a kind of territorial unit. Therefore all land in a single mbari belonged to one man's descendants. The mbari was responsible for land distribution to the Kikuyu members.

The clan system promoted unity among the Kikuyu. In fact the mbari system could have developed into a very powerful centralised system of government if the British had not interfered with it during the colonial period.

The Hehe

The name 'Hehe' never existed before the arrival of whitemen in East Africa. The name was coined by the Europeans to refer to various ethnic groups like the Usagara, Ubena and Ukimbu who used to shout 'Hee! Hee! Hee!' when going into battle.

In the 18th century, there were more than fifteen chiefdoms, which remained separate and independent until the 19th century. They however shared certain things, such as burying dead chiefs and throwing away dead commoners. A living man was buried in a sitting position with a dead chief, and he supported the head of the dead body.

The Ntemi chiefs had a great role to play in those societies. The Hehe people believed that they carried the spirits of the former chiefs. So the Ntemi were deeply feared. They were also believed to have potent war medicines.

During the 19th century, two leaders of the Hehe people emerged. These leaders surrounded themselves with a lot of power and pomp. These were Chief Manyigumba and his son, Mkwawa.

Revision 9

1. (a) Describe the origins of the Nyamwezi.

   (b) How was Nyamwezi society organised by 1850?

2. Describe the social, political and economic organisation of the following:-

   (a) Kikuyu

   (b) Maasai

   (c) Hehe

   (d) Chagga

   (e) Nandi

3. (a) Explain the relationships between the Maasai and the Kikuyu during the 19th century.

   (b) What led to the decline of Maasai power and influence?

4. Describe the way of life of two of the following:

   (a) Maasai (Kwavi)

   (b) Chagga

   (c) Kikuyu

10

The Ngoni invasion of East Africa

The Ngoni were part of the Nguni speaking people of South Africa. They formed part of the Bantu. They are related to the Zulu people of South Africa. Originally, they lived around the area now known as Natal. Their migration from South Africa to East Africa was the last wave of the Bantu migration which took place in the 19th century.

Reasons for the Ngoni migration

Several reasons were responsible for the Ngoni migration into East Africa in the 19th century.

- *Overpopulation:* This was attributed to the fertile land around Natal. As food production increased as a result of the introduction of maize in the area by the Portuguese in the 15th century, people increased in number. So there was need for more land.

- *Lack of land:* As a result of overpopulation the little land left had to be competed for. Consequently stronger societies occupied more and more land while the weaker societies, such as the Ngoni, had to move elsewhere.

- *Fear of the Mfecane (time of troubles):* This was set in motion by Shaka Zulu of South Africa. Shaka was a feared king who did not spare the life of whoever opposed him. Several societies, including the Ngoni, left South Africa to look for vacant land where they could be free from Shaka's tyranny.

The course of their migration

The Ngoni people were led by a man called Zwangendaba. They started their journey from south of River Limpopo and plundered Mashonaland in around 1831. They also destroyed the former kingdom of Monomotapa as they moved. They crossed the Zambezi river near Zambo in 1835. Thereafter they defeated the Cewa people of present-day Malawi. The Maseko Ngoni took the eastern direction and settled in Songea.

Zwangendaba took his group to the Ufipa Plateau where he settled and established his kingdom. He had learnt of the red cattle in the neighbourhood. When the Ngoni reached the Ufipa Plateau, they found a loosely organised tribe called Fipa whom they defeated easily and over whom they established their hegemony. Zwangendaba died on the Ufipa Plateau in 1848.

Shaka Zulu

Ngoni in Ufipa Plateau

After the death of Zwangendaba, rivalry over leadership became serious as every prince wanted to take over. As a result of this dynastic rivalry, the Ngoni split into five main groups, two of which remained in East Africa.

Three groups of the Ngoni returned south, raiding Zambia and Malawi. The group led by Mpenzeni settled in the highlands and Fort Johnson. The Tuta Ngoni moved northwards into Holoholo territory. They fought and defeated the Holoholo once, but the Holoholo adopted a new system of warfare and they defeated the Ngoni invaders. The Ngoni were driven away, after which they settled in the Runzewe district north-west of Tabora. Here the Tuta Ngoni raided and plundered their neighbours. They disrupted the long-distance trade and life among the Nyamwezi as they captured the young and taught them their military tactics. Among the young captives was Mirambo.

Another group, the Gwangwara, was led by Zulu-Gama eastwards to Songea. Here they encountered the Maseko Ngoni led by Maputo who had taken the eastern direction. Because the Maseko Ngoni were a very large and well organised group, at first the Gwangara accepted their leadership, but later war erupted between the two groups. The Maseko Ngoni were defeated, and they fled in disarray. Some Maseko fled across River Ruvuma into Mozambique, while others fled to the Kilombero valley where they became known as Mpuga. Others scattered to Tunduru, Masasi and Newala.

Reasons for Ngoni success

To understand the reasons for the Ngoni success, one must first refer to the early history of the Ngoni in South Africa. As noted earlier, the Ngoni left South Africa owing to fear of Shaka. Shaka Zulu was such a well organised man militarily. He had a well trained army made up of *impis*, or fighting units. The Ngoni became very successful when they inherited Shaka's military tactics.

The Ngoni planned every battle carefully before they got involved in it. They also used weapons different from those of most other people they encountered. For instance, they used assegais (short stabbing spears) instead of the long throwing spears. They also used the 'cowhorn' formation in order to engulf and destroy their enemy.

During their long journey to East Africa, the Ngoni captured young men whom they conscripted into the army and they married young women captives. This did not only increase the number of the Ngoni people, but resulted in their assimilation of captives into Ngoni culture. Furthermore, most of the communities encountered by the Ngoni people were small and disorganised and, as such, they were not strong enough to contain the Ngoni invaders in the wake of the *Mfecane*.

Another important reason for Ngoni success was their courage. Having left their original motherland, they were determined to get a new homeland, whatever resistance they encountered along the way, in order to defend themselves and their property.

Consequences of Ngoni invasion of East Africa

The Ngoni people who entered East Africa in the middle of the 19th century had a profound and long-lasting effect on East Africa. First and foremost, they forced the small African states to unite and form larger states, for instance, states of the Hehe and the Unyamwezi.

- They also incorporated the small African societies like the Fipa into the Ngoni state.

- The local people copied the Ngoni tactics. For instance, the Holoholo defeated the Tuta Ngoni by using the Ngoni's own tactics. The people in Ufipa in the 1850s also challenged the Ngoni.

- Another immediate outcome of the Ngoni invasion was the devastation of many settlements in Tanzania. Many villages were destroyed as a result of the Ngoni invasion.

- The invasion interfered with long-distance trade, thus leading to shortages in areas which had not experienced the presence of the Ngoni.

- As many homes were destroyed and their occupants fled in fear, agriculture was disrupted, leading to famine.

- The Ngoni introduced new military tactics to the people of East Africa, especially those of Tanzania. For instance, the use of the 'cowhorn' formation at the battlefront, the use of assegais, etc.

- They led to the appearance of loose and disorderly groups called Rugaruga and Mviti who were very unruly thugs, smoked opuim and lived by looting and plundering.

- The Ngoni invasion weakened resistance of Africans to the slave traders as their solidarity was destroyed by the invaders.

- The Ngoni invasion led to the depopulation of East Africa as many people were killed during the wars.

- The Ngoni invasion also led to untold suffering of people as many parents were killed, leaving behind orphans without people to care for them.

- The Ngoni invasion of East Africa also led to the rise of important men like Mirambo and Nyungu ya Mawe.

- Many people fled in disarray, and a large number of them became completely destribalised.

- The Ngoni invasion was partly responsible for Europe's success in imposing colonial rule on the peoples of East Africa as they had already been weakened.

Revision 10

1 Who were the Ngoni?

2 (a) Describe the migration and settlement of the Ngoni peoples into East Africa.

   (b) Why were the Ngoni successful in their invasion of East Africa?

3 (a) Describe the course of the Ngoni migration into eastern Africa between 1820 and 1860.

   (b) How did this migration affect the peoples of mainland Tanganyika?

4 (a) Why was the Ngoni invasion of the settled communities of East Africa in the mid 19th century successful?

(b) What were the effects of this invasion on Tanzania?

11

Some notable East African leaders

Mirambo

Like many men in history who attain greatness, Mirambo had very humble beginnings. Born in 1830, he was a Nyamwezi by birth. Then he was captured by the Ngoni invaders. He spent the greater part of his early life with the Ngoni as a captive. While among the Ngoni people, he acquired the military knowledge and skills of the Ngoni people which he later used to great advantage.

He also gained experience in trade, especially the caravan trade which had been going on around him. After acquiring the war tactics of the Ngoni, Mirambo organised a very strong and well paid army called *rugaruga*. The rugaruga became the real basis of Mirambo's administration.

It did not take long before Mirambo was recognised as a power to reckon with. He started out as a small ruler of Uyowa or Ugowe. He later acquired Uliankuru from his mother's family. After acquiring those two chiefdoms, Mirambo launched expeditions against his neighbours. During the 1860s and 1870s, Mirambo organised expeditions against the Vinza, Tongwe, Nyaturu, Irambo, Sumbwa and the Sukuma. By 1876, Mirambo had established a renowned capital city, Urambo, in his kingdom. It was a big market which competed favourably with the Arab-controlled Unyanyembe market.

Mirambo's kingdom was called Unyamwezi. By 1880, Mirambo controlled a territory which was crossed by the caravan routes from the coast to southern Uganda, Burundi and Rwanda.

Mirambo's success in building his empire owed much to his unique personality. He had a character which was quite rare: he could clearly see what he was trying to achieve.

Secondly, Mirambo had unlimited energy. He was so strong that he always beat all his opponents in a fight.

Mirambo, just like his captors, the Ngoni, absorbed his conquered enemies and recruited their youths into his army. This helped Mirambo to become very powerful in East Africa.

Mirambo was so wise a man that he commanded respect from the Arabs who crossed his empire to trade. They had to honour him as a leader.

Mirambo was very courageous and always personally led his army into battle. Mirambo had about 500 well-trained and armed mercenaries. He had another seven thousand warriors who were as courageous as himself.

Mirambo's achievements

- His first achievement was his rise to power from slave status.

- Mirambo organised the rugaruga whom he used to expand his empire which came to be known as Unyamwezi.

- Mirambo was a very successful trader who came to be recognised by the famous Tippu Tip and Sultan Barghash of Zanzibar. Initially, the Arabs refused to recognise him as a leader, but when he closed the caravan routes, the Arabs sued for peace and accepted his terms. Not only did they recognise him as a leader of Unyamwezi but they also paid taxes for crossing his territory.

- Mirambo also maintained good relations with Europeans. He made them feel welcome to his territory, especially the missionaries, and lived amicably with them.

Mirambo's failures

- Mirambo failed to secure the friendship of the Kabaka of Buganda who had a lot of political influence around the Great Lakes region.

- Mirambo did not create a strong cadre of political leaders. He was autocratic, i.e. all powers were in his hands alone. When he died, his empire did not survive for long. It disintegrated rapidly.

- Under Mirambo's rule, local leaders retained their powers. Apart from Mirambo, there was no other unifying factor in the whole empire.

- Mirambo's mercenaries were not dependable either. They were likely to sell their services to anyone who was willing to pay them well.

- Mirambo's empire had no effective central administration. The result was that when Mirambo died in 1884, his half-brother and successor, Mpandashalo, could not stop the vast empire from collapsing.

However, Mirambo symbolised the reaction of African people to external forces. Even if Mirambo had not died, leading to the collapse of the once renowned Nyamwezi empire, Mirambo's empire was bound to collapse in the hands of the European imperialists who had come to usurp African sovereignty and impose colonial rule.

Nyungu ya Mawe

Nyungu ya Mawe was a son of the Unyanyembe ruling family. When the Arabs murdered Mnwa Sele, the chief of Unyanyembe, by beheading him, Nyungu ya Mawe fled to Kiwele. From Kiwele, around 1870, Nyungu ya Mawe organised many expeditions into areas east and south of Tabora especially in Kimbu country.

During these protracted expeditions, large tracts of land fell to him including the trade routes which joined Tabora to the Ufipa plateau.

All the areas around Lake Tanganyika also fell under his control. After conquering that large area, Nyungu ya Mawe formed a very strong and centralised administration. He appointed his own loyal officials, called *vatwale*, to administer the conquered chiefdoms.

The vatwale had no political rights; all political power was vested in Nyungu ya Mawe. The Vatwale were responsible for the collection of ivory and other valuable trading commodities like iron and gold from the conquered chiefs. All the items collected from the conquered chiefs had to be sent to Nyungu ya Mawe's at his residence in Kiwele.

Nyungu ya Mawe divided his kingdom into seven administrative units and each of them was allocated to a *mutwale* (singular of *vatwale*). The division of the kingdom did not take into account the traditional boundaries of the conquered chiefs. This helped Nyungu ya Mawe's centralised administration to survive for long as his subjects were disunited.

Like Mirambo, Nyungu ya Mawe had a very strong army of mercenaries. They were given thorough physical and psychological training. His mercenaries were reputedly brave professional soldiers who were very ruthless in battle. Nyungu ya Mawe was a man who did not hesitate to risk the lives of his men in order to secure victory. In fact, he always referred to his Rugaruga as *mapimpiti,* i.e. logs. When asking for reinforcements, Nyungu ya Mawe would shout, "Pile on more logs!"

Nyungu's warriors

By 1871 his men had raided south of Unyanyembe. In 1875, the chiefdoms of Nanzi, which included Kirurumo and Kiwele, were occupied. By December 1884, the areas in the southern part of Ukonongo, Wikangulu and many Kimbu chiefdoms were already under his rule. It is believed that Nyungu ya

Mawe's empire lasted longer than that of Mirambo, his contemporary. Since Nyungu ya Mawe did not meet the Europeans, there is limited literature about him.

However, after his death, his daughter ruled the kingdom until she died in 1893. She was in turn succeeded by her daughter. The great empire of Nyungu ya Mawe only started to disintegrate in 1895 when the German imperialists reached Kiwele. The Germans were accepted as the allies of the Unyanyembe and the Hehe and, as such, they did not have to use military force in order to impose their rule. Nevertheless, the Germans replaced the vatwale with their own administrators, the *akidas*. That marked the end of Nyungu ya Mawe's empire.

Munyigumba

Munyigumba came to power between 1855 and 1860. He became the head of the Lungemba chiefdom. As a formidable ruler and a military expert, Munyigumba became so powerful in the area that he extended his administration all over the northern part of Heheland. He further brought the whole of the Hehe plateau and highlands under his control.

Unfortunately he died in 1878 and, for the first time, all his conquered territory did not have one supreme ruler. However, he was replaced by his son, Mkwawa, whose character was similar to that of his father and who also favoured an expansionist policy.

The rule of Mkwawa

He was not different from his father, Munyigumba. Immediately after succeeding his father, Mkwawa greatly expanded the inherited kingdom. He fought the Gogo in the north and the Usagara in the north-east. He conquered this northern territory in order to control the trade routes which passed through it. By 1880, the Hehe had become so powerful under Mkwawa that they posed a big threat to the caravan traders.

After establishing his control and consolidating his power over the conquered areas, Mkwawa became a formidable monarch with a well fortified city in Kalanga. When German colonialists came to Tanganyika, Mkwawa put up a stiff resistance to the German invaders. There was no way the Germans could disregard him. They had to respect his independence.

Revision 11

1   Describe the career and achievements of the following:-

    (a)   Nyungu ya Mawe

    (b)   Mirambo

    (c)   Mkwawa

2   Show how Mkwawa responded to the colonial occupation of his areas.

3   Describe the social, political and economic organisation of the Nyamwezi empire under the rule of Mirambo.

12

Internal trade in East Africa

The decision made by Sayyid Said to move his capital from Muscat to Zanzibar has been praised by historians because it encouraged long-distance trade in East Africa. For the first time, Zanzibar became an important terminus for international trade between East Africa and the outside world.

Unlike other Muslims who preferred wars to peaceful negotiations with 'infidels', Sayyid Said was quite different. He wanted to ally himself with the powers of the Indian Ocean, notably the British. Sayyid Said saw a great need to put the caravan trade on a better footing; so he encouraged the traders from the coast to travel inland. The need for slaves was also increasing as the Arabs had acquired land and had opened large clove plantations; so there was need to go inland and acquire them.

The Indian traders, commonly known as *Banyans*, had been encouraged to come to East Africa, especially to Zanzibar, by Sayyid Said. They provided the necessary financial backing and also supplied the goods necessary for the caravans. The *Banyans* were not only traders; they also lent money to the traders, for which they charged colossal amounts of money as interest. In addition, they also collected customs duties from the traders who passed through Zanzibar.

Some Europeans were allowed to settle in Zanzibar, which became a flourishing centre of commerce and business and a meeting place of all kinds of people.

Long-distance trade
Items of trade
The following goods were very important in the East African long-distance trade: cloth, beads, brassware, gunpowder, guns, and provisions for caravans. All these items were imported to

East Africa from the European countries; whereas the region exported slaves, ivory, cloves, rubber, cowrie shells, gum copal, sesame seed, maize and millet.

Trade routes

There were about four main trade routes in East Africa. One of them, running from Sudan through northern Uganda, was under the control of the 'Khartoumers'. These traders were the subjects of the Khedive of Egypt. Others were the northern, central and the southern routes.

a) ***The northern route:*** This route led from Pangani, Tanga and Mombasa inland to the Kilimanjaro and Taita area. It was divided into two parts. From Kilimanjaro one route ran due west to the eastern shores of Lake Victoria. Then another route ran north-westwards to Mt Kenya, Lake Baringo and Lake Turkana, and across the Rift Valley as far as the slopes of Mt. Elgon.

b) ***The central route:*** This route started from the Mrima coast, which is opposite Zanzibar island, from ports like Bagamoyo and Saadani and cut through Zaramo and Gogo country to Tabora in Unyanyembe. From Unyanyembe, it divided into three different branches:

   (i)   One route ran north-westwards to Karagwe, Buganda and Bunyoro.

   (ii) Another one ran due west to Ujiji on Lake Tanganyika and on to western Zaire.

   (iii) And a third route ran south-west, round the shores of Lake Tanganyika towards Katanga.

(c) ***The southern route:*** This route ran from ports like Kilwa and Malindi inland through the country of the Yao, the Makua and the Makonde to Lake Malawi. This was the principal route for the export of slaves and it was dominated by the Yao people.

The participants in long-distance trade

There were three main groups of participants in the long-distance caravan trade of East Africa; they were the Arabs at the coast, Swahili traders and the Africans. There were only three African groups who participated. These were the Nyamwezi, the Yao and the Kamba.

Arabs and Swahili (Zanzibaris)

As we have already seen, Sayyid Said began sending caravans into the interior of East Africa in the mid 1830s. He realised very early that there was need to make friends with the people of the interior, especially the Nyamwezi who were very powerful. In 1839, he made a treaty with a leading merchant prince, Chief Fundikira of Unyanyembe. This treaty allowed the Arab traders to pass through Unyanyembe and to trade in Unyamwezi without paying taxes. The Arab and Swahili traders therefore gradually increased in number and eventually built their own centre outside the capital. This centre became known as Kezeh and later, Tabora.

Tabora became the centre of Arab and Swahili trade in the interior with routes leading south to Konongo and Fipa, north to Usukuma, Uzinza and Lake Victoria, and north-west to Karagwe, Buganda and later to Bunyoro. Another route led to Ujiji and the Congo. A number of Arab and Swahili traders, commonly called Zanzibaris, also built houses in Tabora, settled permanently and became very wealthy.

The Arabs became very powerful and wealthy. When Mnwa Sele, a new Nyamwezi ruler, tried to oppose the Arab traders, he was defeated and driven away from his own kingdom. He is believed to have attacked the Arabs frequently, but he failed to regain his chiefdom. Many people supported the Arabs and both sides used the Rugaruga in their wars. These wars accelerated the slave trade as many of the war captives were sold as slaves.

Ivory was one of the lucrative items and was in very high demand in Europe and America. It was used to make valuable items like piano keys, knife handles, buttons and billiard balls. This commodity was carried from the interior by either hired slaves or other Africans who wanted clothes. The Nyamwezi were excellent porters because they used to walk long distances carrying the heavy tusks.

The Arabs also took many slaves, especially women and children, to the coast. Due to the Ngoni invasion and the rise of new leaders like Mirambo and Nyungu ya Mawe, the situation in the interior became fluid. The Arabs, who were already very powerful, exploited this situation and started using force to get women, children, food, men and animals.

The Arabs and Swahili treated the captives badly and usually about two thirds of these captives died before they reached the coast.

Nyamwezi

Nyamwezi country in central Tanzania was intersected by trade routes. Accordingly, the Nyamwezi took advantage of this to become prominent porters and traders in the region.

Nyamwezi skills in trading and porterage became status symbols. A good background in trade and porterage was a ladder to becoming a chief among the Nyamwezi people.

The Nyamwezi also took advantage of the demand for iron ore from Usangi and Mtunze, copper from Katanga and salt from Uvinza in the north-west.

The Nyamwezi began to be involved in ivory trade towards the end of the 18th century. By 1800 the first Nyamwezi caravan arrived at the coast with ivory. The increased demand for ivory exports in India, Europe and North America in the 19th century stimulated the expansion of ivory trade.

Trade became an essential part of Nyamwezi life and society. By the 1830s large Nyamwezi caravans, each consisting of about one thousand Nyamwezi people, had begun to arrive regularly at the coast with their loads of merchandise such as ivory, slaves and wax. They stayed at the coast in large encampments, trading and farming until the next dry season. Then they returned home carrying cloth, beads and other trade goods.

The Nyamwezi travelled further inland, venturing as far as Katanga, Buganda and even eastern Congo. As a result of Arab-

Nyamwezi rivalry, the trade route in central Tanzania became very busy, with traders jostling with one another to increase their share of the lucrative trade and to maximise profits. Under powerful leaders like Mirambo and Nyungu ya Mawe, the Nyamwezi people continuously played a major role in the organisation of long-distance trade in the 19th century. The central trade route became very famous even to the European travellers who came to East Africa then. It was along this route that new crops like maize, rice and cassava were first introduced.

It has been said that the Nyamwezi themselves became more cosmopolitan in their outlook and started to lose their kinship attachments. Respect given for the old system disappeared and people became loyal to caravan groups, hunters' guilds or secret societies such as Baswezi and Wayeye (snake experts).

The copper the Nyamwezi brought from Katanga was often used as a kind of currency alongside the copper bangles and ornaments which were made by the Ha and the Sumbwa. By the 1850s, the Nyamwezi had established their trading posts on the far side of Lake Tanganyika. Ngelengwa, commonly known as Msiri, settled in Katanga and because of his vast wealth established his own empire.

It is worth noting that the Nyamwezi also got involved in slave trade in the interior. People like the Gogo, who were pastoralists, needed slaves to work on their farms, so they exchanged ivory for slaves with the Nyamwezi. The Nyamwezi were able to intensify slave trade after the arrival of guns from the coast.

The Yao
The Yao were the major long-distance traders from the south. They loved travelling, just like the Nyamwezi. The Yao were probably the most active slave traders in the 19th century in East Africa. They were among the first people to develop long-distance trade. Originally, they were agriculturalists who wanted hoes and other implements whose production was a monopoly of the Cisi. These ironsmiths moved around Yao land selling their products. Around the 16th and 17th

centuries, the Arabs started to trade with the Yao in items like cloth, beads, brassware, etc. The Yao's involvement in slave trade only started around the middle of the 19th century when the Ngoni invasion disrupted trade. War captives were sold as slaves. The Yao took advantage of the confusion brought about by the Makua to intensify their involvement in the slave trade. The Yao commitment to slave trade gained momentum in response to the demand for increased slaves at the coast, especially around the Kilwa ports.

Under the influence of powerful leaders like Mpanda, Mataka, Machemba and Mtalika, the Yao dominated the southern trade route. No other group of traders was powerful enough to challenge the Yao dominance. Even coastal traders became clients of these rulers; they brought guns, beads, glass and other items such as clothes which they bartered for slaves. The Yao became so powerful that both Arabs and Swahili could not pass through their country without permission. The Yao were very hostile to European intrusion in the region because they feared that intruders would jeopardise their profitable way of life.

The Kamba
The Kamba were the most vigorous long-distance traders in what is now called Kenya. They were living in an area which had very unreliable rainfall. Their ancestors therefore lived in small groups, surviving on hunting and shifting cultivation around the Mbooni Hills. Their trading activities began when they started bartering elephant tusks with the Nyika for cattle.

By the early 19th century, the Kamba people had developed a very complex trading system. They supplied their neighbours with meat, grain and beer; they also traded in arrowheads and iron ornaments. The Kamba merchants expanded their trade northwards towards Samburu and southwards towards Uzaramo.

Originally, the Kamba people were not involved in slave trade, but later as they grew rich, they started buying slaves to use as domestic workers. Slave raiding only became really important to the Kamba when they started travelling very far away from their homes in search of ivory. Slaves were needed to carry the ivory.

Among the Kamba traders, Kivoi was very famous. He made a name for himself in the 1830s and 1840s as a great hunter and trader. Chief Kivoi had an enormous number of followers and slaves whom he organised into a caravan around Kilimanjaro and beyond Mt Kenya. Kivoi controlled the trade between the Kamba and Kikuyu and he exacted taxes from the neighbouring Maasai.

However, Kamba dominance did not last beyond 1870. By 1870 their influence had started to decline owing to the increasing scarcity of ivory. Furthermore, the Arabs and Swahili were busy organising their own caravans to the north-west in Kikuyu and Embu. The highland people who had been exploited by the Kamba now wanted direct trade with the coast, partly in protest against Kamba slave raids. Nevertheless, the Kamba, like Nyamwezi, remained influential in the long-distance trade up to the colonial period.

Tippu Tip

Tippu Tip is the most widely known slave and ivory dealer in the whole of Africa. He was born to Mohammed bin Juma and Mrima in 1830. Mrima was an African from the East Coast. Tippu Tip looked more like an African than an Arab. His full name was Mohammed bin Hamid. His father lived mostly in the interior of East Africa. Tippu Tip's father had been a trader owning a plantation near Tabora. In about 1850 Tippu Tip was assisting his father in the Tabora area.

As soon as he was old enough, he started his own business. He later joined his friend Said bin Omar. He thereafter started going into the interior of Tanzania until he reached Nsamba's kingdom of Ruemba.

Tippu Tip led many expeditions around the Lake Tanganyika region. In 1865, he reached Ruemba on the eastern shore of Lake Tanganyika where he seized the local chief's supply of ivory and he installed his brother Mohammed bin Masad as the local ruler. With his pragmatic military qualities, great negotiation skills and diplomatic appearance, Tippu Tip entered Congo through the area south of Lake Tanganyika. There he befriended Runga Kabari, king of the Rua.

Tippu Tip, Afro-Arab slave trader

Because he looked friendly and loyal, the Rua people thought that he would live with them cordially, but it did not take long before Tippu Tip turned against them and conquered them. The Rua King was reinstated on condition that he provided Tippu Tip with guides to the ivory zone. As a result, he was guided to Manyama where a lot of ivory could be obtained. Just south of Rualand lived chief Kosongo - Ruchie who had been a target of attacks from the Rua. Kosongo's own sisters had been captured and sold as slaves.

Tippu Tip deceived Kosongo that he was his grandson, that he was the son of one of the sisters who had been sold into slavery by the Rua. Kosongo then stepped down in favour of Tippu Tip. When Kosongo relinquished power to Tippu Tip, he had already created an empire. Tippu Tip, with the support of 40,000 people, started ruling the empire. He expanded his rule to Nyangwe.

By 1883, Tippu Tip's name had spread as far as Stanley Falls. Almost a quarter of River Congo had fallen under his rule by 1890. Tippu Tip appointed about fifteen of his relatives to control the far-flung areas of his dominion. Tippu Tip established trade relations with men like Mirambo of the Unyamwezi empire and Rumaliza of Ujiji. In the end, Tippu Tip became a well known cosmopolitan trader whose fame extended from Congo to the East African coast.

When the Europeans were partitioning Africa, part of Tippu Tip's empire fell into the hands of the king of Belgium, Leopold II, in 1887. When Stanley arrived in Zanzibar, he offered Tippu Tip the governorship of Stanley Falls. Tippu Tip started receiving a salary and he was permitted to trade in anything he liked apart from slaves.

In 1890, Tippu Tip left one of his nephews in charge of Stanley Falls and reached Zanzibar in 1891. During his absence from Congo things started going wrong and the Belgians defeated the Arabs. This marked the end of Arab influence in Congo. Tippu Tip died in Zanzibar in 1905 without going back to claim his dominion in Congo.

Trade in Buganda

The Baganda were among the most active traders in East Africa by the second half of the 19th century. This trade gained a lot of momentum in Buganda when the Arab and Swahili traders arrived there. Among the trading items which the Baganda valued highly were cloth, beads and guns. They also wanted the help of the traders against their neighbours, the Basoga and Banyoro. In fact, in 1848 the Arabs helped them fight the Basoga.

The Baganda supplied the Arabs with ivory and slaves and many other goods. There was a very clear pattern in this trade. The Sultan of Zanzibar was represented in the Kabaka's court so that the visiting traders could carry on with their trade unhindered. The Arabs provided the Baganda with guns which were used to raid slaves from neighbouring territories. The raids were carried out in Ankole, Busoga, Toro, Bunyoro,

Buvuma and Ukerewe islands on Lake Victoria. They also raided western Kenya. Because of this trade, the Kabaka and Buganda grew very rich and powerful. The Baganda forbade the Arabs and Swahili from going to Bunyoro for fear that the Banyoro would be supplied with guns and defeat them.

Revision 12

1 (a) How was long - distance trade in East Africa organised between 1800 and 1880?

   (b) What effects did it have on the peoples of East Africa?

2 (a) Describe the organisation of the long - distance trade in East Africa.

   (b) What were the effects of this trade on the people of East Africa?

3 (a) What was the long - distance trade in East Africa during the 19th century?

   (b) Describe the origins and the extent of the three main trade routes in this long - distance trade.

4 (a) How was trade on the East African coast organised by 1500 AD?

   (b) What were the effects of this trade on the East African coast during this period?

13

Slave trade in East Africa

Slavery is the owning of human beings by fellow human beings. Slaves were forced to work for their owners without being paid for their work. Slavery existed in many societies in Africa. This was because of inter-tribal wars. The victorious tribe always took home prisoners of war who became domestic servants or slaves. Other people were also exchanged for food items among the Africans. Whenever there was famine, it was common practice for people to barter their children for food.

On the other hand, slave trade is the transaction in human beings. This involves the capture, transportation and sale of human beings. In East Africa, slave trade had been in existence for a long time. From the available evidence, mainly from accounts written by early traders from Greece, slave trade existed at the coast as long ago as during the first AD. However, slave trade increased tremendously in East Africa in the second half of the 18th century, i.e. between 1759 and 1800.

Reasons for the intensification of slave trade (18th - 19th centuries)

Several factors were responsible for the escalation of slave trade in East Africa during the two centuries.

- The demand for slaves to work in the French plantations on Reunion and Mauritius islands in the Indian Ocean was high. The French had established themselves in Malagasy where they had plantations and needed slaves to work on them. The Frenchmen could not work in their plantations there because the climate of the islands was too harsh for them, and they believed that the only people who could work there successfully were the Africans.

These Africans were obtained from East Africa as slaves.

- When the British abolished slave trade in 1807 in Britain and later in their territories overseas, they stationed their warships in the Atlantic Ocean and on the coast of West Africa in order to check the transportation of slaves from West Africa across the ocean. This created a problem for the Portuguese who had plantations in Brazil. They therefore turned to East and Central Africa for the slaves. This increased the demand for slaves and slave trade thrived between 1760 and 1856.

- At that time, the French and Portuguese demand for slaves was very high in East Africa. Secondly the Omani Arabs and the Swahili people were already well established in East Africa. They therefore took advantage of this demand and began raiding for slaves.

- After the transfer of his capital to Zanzibar, Sayyid Said established clove and coconut plantations in Zanzibar. These plantations needed workers to maintain them. Therefore, the slaves became very important. Slaves were thus raided and sold both to the foreigners and the families at the coast of East Africa.

- The increase in slave trade was also partly due to the increase in the demand for slaves in north-east Africa, Arabia and Persia. It is important to note that the above countries had traded in slaves from East Africa for a very long time.

- Another factor which helped to intensify slave trade in East Africa was the transfer of Sayyid Said's capital from Muscat to Zanzibar. The slave trade increased because the Omani Arabs opened the trade route into the interior of East Africa. By 1839 between forty and forty-five thousand slaves were being sold in the Zanzibar slave market every year. By the 1860s the slave cargo had increased to seventy thousand people.

How the slaves were obtained

The slaves came to the Zanzibar market from several East African areas. Guns played a major role in the slave raids. In East Africa, there were three major ways by which the slaves were obtained. One was direct purchase from the local rulers. These rulers often disposed of their war captives, the social misfits, criminals or destitutes by selling them off as slaves. In exchange for those slaves they received guns and other valuable trading articles like mirrors, ornaments, cloth, etc. For example, the Gogo captured Africans and exchanged them for those goods.

Secondly, the slave dealers used the tactic of inciting rulers to wage war against their neighbours. During these wars, the slave raiders, mainly Arabs and Swahili, rendered military assistance. They afterwards took a share of the war booty as a reward for the military service rendered.

Lastly, the slaves were obtained through direct attack by the slave dealers using guns. The slave dealers raided the disunited tribes, burning houses and killing those who tried to resist. All the young men, women and children were enslaved. The raids were usually carried out at night. The slaves began by setting houses on fire and as the occupants fled for their lives, they were captured by the Arab slave raiders.

During their transportation, slaves were treated brutally.

- They were chained together with a strong rope to a *goree* stick.

- They were made to walk while the Arabs who drove the slaves rode on horses and donkeys.

- Any slow-moving slave would be flogged.

- Those who were too weak to walk were killed and left on the way. David Livingstone saw some corpses which were left on the trade route by the Arab slave dealers and described it thus: 'We passed a woman tied by the neck to a tree and dead. We saw others ... tied up in similar manner and one lying in the path shot or stabbed, for she was in a pool of blood.'

- The sick were left to die on the way.
- Even the slaves in chains were made to carry ivory.

Because of this brutal treatment of the Africans by the Arabs, only one third of the slaves taken from the interior reached the coast; and for every slave captured, ten people might have been killed.

The slaves were taken to Kilwa and Zanzibar where they were dressed and fed before they were taken to the slave markets to be sold. The feeding and dressing was done for commercial purposes because good-looking slaves fetched more money than naked, miserable-looking ones. These slaves sold in Zanzibar were mostly taken to the Middle East whereas those sold at Kilwa were exported to Reunion and Brazil.

The Khartoumers

These were the Egyptians and Sudanese slave traders who came to East Africa from the north. They entered East Africa through the northern part of present-day Uganda. They were the most brutal slave and ivory traders who plundered and killed many people during the slave trade in northern Uganda. They first arrived in East Africa around the 1820s when the Egyptians started pushing their border southwards into Sudan. Whenever the Egyptians conquered any area, the traders were the first people to arrive there.

When the Khartoumers, many of whom were criminals who had been released from jail ,came to northern Uganda, they found a lot of elephants there. They incited one community against another in order to acquire cattle to exchange for ivory. All these activities caused a lot of problems in northern Uganda. The Khartoumers even started capturing slaves to carry their ivory for them. The only people who survived their manoeuvres were the Langi who repulsed the Khartoumers when they entered Lango country. The activities of the Khartoumers only came to an end when the Mahdi rose against the Egyptians and cut off the route to northern Uganda.

The impact of slave trade on the people of East Africa

The slave trade, which lasted many centuries in East Africa, had far-reaching effects that fundamentally altered the lives of East Africans. Apart from immediate human suffering and misery, it had a profound political, economic and social impact.

Political

This trade strengthened the large and powerful states at the expense of the weaker ones owing to the fact that they had easy access to guns. Secondly, there was a move away from small political units, i.e. clan units, to larger units under one leadership for defence purposes. For instance, Mirambo built the Unyamwezi empire out of small chiefdoms.

Thirdly, the slave trade broke down the clan and tribal units and disrupted inter-tribal peace as tribe would turn against tribe and clan against clan in search of slaves.

Fourthly, the trade led to the death of the people who would have been leaders and empire builders. In one way or another, the slave trade hindered political development in East Africa.

Lastly, power shifted from the traditional hereditary leaders to non-hereditary leaders who were ambitious and courageous, e.g. Nyungu ya Mawe and Mirambo.

Economic

The slave trade led to the prosperity of some individuals and tribes such as the Kamba. They profited a great deal from the trade. Secondly, the trade brought a new kind of livelihood to many Africans. Many people who used to depend on peasant agriculture got involved in the trade and became prosperous. New food crops like cloves and coconuts were introduced through this trade and flourishing plantations were established around the trading centres.

The slave trade also led to the growth of towns such as Tabora, Kilwa and Zanzibar. The slave trade led to suffering and human misery as some people, especially the old, were left without care. Some people fled in disarray for their lives and started living in the bushes without their parents and relatives, neglecting agriculture. Hence many people died from hunger.

Farmlands were deserted resulting in decline in food production and security. Famine, poverty and destitution became the order of the day as many crops were devastated by the slave raiders. African arts and crafts were destroyed since the imported European goods began to be preferred to the locally manufactured goods.

Those Africans who had engaged in the slave trade for long found themselves jobless and became criminals when it was abolished.

Social

The slave trade in East Africa also had some social effects. It led to depopulation as many people died during the slave raids and others were exported outside Africa. Many people who survived the slave trade lost their relatives, children, parents and friends. The slaves themselves suffered a great deal, and sometimes died, from being beaten and yoked together with the *goree* stick. With the disintegration of African communities, many victims of the slave trade became homeless and lost their ethnic and cultural identify. In other words, they were detribalised.

Many people were also detribalised as a result of running away from their homes, while others became homeless.

The abolition of slave trade

The idea of abolishing slave trade started in Britain and spread to other parts of the world. It must be noted that Britain had been the main slave - trading nation in the world until 1807 when slave trade was declared illegal in Britain. In 1833, it was declared illegal in British overseas territories.

The move to abolish slave trade and slavery was started by humanitarians such as Lord Chief Justice Mansfield, who declared that slave trade was illegal according to British law, and Adam Smith who denounced slave labour as being more expensive than free labour in his book *The Wealth of Nations*.

Men like Pitt, the leader of the Conservative Party, and William Wilberforce condemned slave trade publicly in the British Parliament. Other prominent people who denounced slave trade were Thomas Clarkson, who wrote an essay condemning it in 1807, and John Wesley and his Methodist followers. All these people helped immensely in stopping slave trade.

Another reason for stopping slave trade was that it had become less profitable for the British. The British had to persuade other nations to accept to abolish slave trade. Portugal stopped slave trade in 1815, France prohibited it in 1818, and Spain in 1820.

Steps taken to abolish slave trade in East Africa

In East Africa, one of the steps which led to the abolition of slave trade was taken in 1815 when the British gained control of Mauritius and the Seychelles islands. The British stopped slavery on those islands and they set up anti-slavery patrol bases there in order to check the transportation of slaves by slave dealers in the Indian Ocean.

The Sultan of Oman, Sayyid Said, who was deeply interested in slave trade, was left in a dilemma. He did not want to lose British friendship but at the same time, he could not stop slave trade for fear of losing a lucrative source of revenue.

The Moresby Treaty

Captain Fairfax Moresby was a governor of Mauritius. He exerted a lot of pressure to convince Sayyid Said to sign a treaty in June 1822 known as the Moresby Treaty. Sayyid Said signed the treaty on September 22, 1822. The main aims of the treaty were:

(i) To prevent Africans from East Africa from being sent outside the Sultan's territories and the Muslim lands of Arabia and Persia.

(ii) To stop the French from carrying the slaves from East Africa to Mauritius and Reunion or to India.

(iii) To encourage what they called legitimate trade.

(iv) To authorise the British to search the ships or dhows suspected of carrying slaves and also to deal with smugglers.

However, the 1822 treaty did not abolish the slave trade but merely limited its sphere of operation. Furthermore, the Indian Ocean was too big for the four British naval patrols to enforce the treaty.

Sayyid Said did not honour Moresby's signature. He violated the treaty and allowed his people to sell slaves wherever they wanted. Neither did the French abide by the treaty. They continued to transport slaves to Reunion. In order to close these loopholes, Said was persuaded by Colonel Hammerton to sign a new treaty – the Hammerton Treaty – in 1845.

The Hammerton Treaty
The Hammerton Treaty was aimed at:
(i) Ending all export of slaves from Zanzibar to Oman.

(ii) Entirely cutting off the slave supplies to the Red Sea.

(iii) Stopping slaves from being exported or sold northwards beyond Brava on the Mogadishu coast.

However, just as the Moresby Treaty failed, so did the Hammerton Treaty. Firstly the Indian Ocean was too vast for the British warships to control. Secondly, the slave traders were always well-armed. Therefore, they resisted efforts to stop their profitable business. Thirdly, the death of Sayyid Said and Hammerton in 1856 and 1857, respectively was a major blow to the enforcement of the treaty. Fourthly, since the freed slaves did not understand the language of the abolitionists, it became difficult to resettle and prevent their re-enslavement.

The Frere Treaty
Around 1871, the British effort to abolish slave trade at the East African coast gained a lot of momentum. As a result, the British set up a commission of inquiry in 1871 to see how the abolition of slave trade could be speeded up.

In 1873, Frere, who was an ex-governor of Bombay, was sent to East Africa to persuade Sultan Barghash to sign a new treaty. The Sultan was reluctant to sign the treaty since the cornerstone of his economy was the slave trade.

In 1872 a hurricane had swept the island, devastating clove plantations, shipping and buildings. Anything aimed at abolishing slave trade would therefore spark off hostility from the Arab slave dealers. Besides, Frere's sharp and abrupt manner did not please the Sultan. Frere left after warning the Sultan that if the treaty was not signed immediately, the British navy would blockade Zanzibar, i.e. stop ships entering or leaving Zanzibar. As a result of this threat, the Sultan had no choice but to sign the treaty on March 1873. In the afternoon of the same day, the Zanzibar slave market was closed.

The terms of the treaty

(i) All public slave markets in the Sultan's dominion were to be closed.

(ii) The Sultan was to protect all the freed slaves.

(iii) The exportation of all slaves was to be stopped forthwith.

(iv) The British were granted powers to check people who wanted to acquire slaves or those who were already in possession of slaves.

In 1876, Barghash declared illegal the transportation of slaves in land caravans. In addition, an agreement was reached, in September 1889, that all persons entering the Sultan's dominion after 1st November 1889 had to be free and that all children born after 1 January 1890 were free. In 1891, the Sultan ordered that the slave trade be prohibited. If a slave owner died without leaving behind any lawful children, all the slaves he owned were to be set free.

The slaves were allowed to bring their complaints to the *Khadi* (magistrate) if they were mistreated. Any case of mistreatment by the master would earn the slave his freedom. The slave trade was completely abolished in Zanzibar and Pemba in 1897 and, in 1911, a decree was issued which disallowed compensation of the slave owners.

On their part, the Germans started killing the slave traders by firing squad in 1888 in Tanganyika, but people still continued trading in slaves until the British, who took over Tanganyika after the First World War, abolished the slave business in 1921.

Revision 13

1 (a) Describe the steps taken by the British to abolish slave trade in East Africa.

(b) What were the results of the abolition of slave trade in East Africa?

2 (a) Why did slave trade intensify in East Africa between the 18th *and 19th* centuries?

(b) How were the slaves obtained?

3 (a) What was the impact of slave trade on the peoples of East Africa?

(b) Why was the slave trade abolished in East Africa?

4 What were the aims of:-

(a) the Moresby Treaty?

(b) the Hammerton Treaty?

(c) the Frere Treaty?

14

European missionaries and explorers in East Africa

The people of the East African interior began coming into contact with Europeans in the middle of the 19th century, i.e. from around 1845. The first Europeans who came to East Africa were missionaries, followed by travellers and traders.

Missionaries

Christian missionaries from Europe came to East Africa to convert Africans to Christianity. There were several reasons for their coming to East Africa in the mid 19th century. The missionaries had already been influenced by the industrial revolution. Besides wishing to spread Christianity, they also wanted to promote trade.

The European Christian revival inspired the missionaries to come not only to East Africa but also to other parts of Africa by the middle of the 19th century. Furthermore, they wanted to help in stopping the slave trade in East Africa. They also wanted to establish legitimate trade to replace the inhuman slave trade.

At that time, Islam was spreading rapidly not only in East Africa but in other parts of Africa as well, so the missionaries came purposely to pre-empt and, if possible, stop the spread of Islam by promoting Christianity.

The missionaries also wanted to promote the growth of cash crops like cotton, coffee, tea, etc. for their home industries. That is why around all their mission stations in East Africa, there were plantations of cash crops.

Missionary work at the coast

The Church Missionary Society (CMS) of England was the first missionary group to bring missionaries to East Africa. The first missionary in East Africa was Dr Ludwig Krapf, a German, who was brought by the CMS. Krapf first worked among the Galla in Ethiopia in 1837 but he was not successful. So in 1844 he went to Zanzibar.

He obtained permission from Sayyid Said to carry out missionary work there. He proceeded to Mombasa and later established a mission station, commonly called Rabai Mission Station, about 24 kilometres from Mombasa.

In due course, Rabai gained a lot of prominence. The first mission school offering the kind of education found in Europe was started there. In July 1848, Krapf visited Usambara where the Shambaa Kimweri Ya Nyumbai invited the missionaries to come and teach his people. In 1849, Krapf travelled through Ukambani where he met Chief Kivoi. The same journey took him up to Mt Kenya, and Krapf became the first white man to see the snow-capped mountain. The following year, 1851, Krapf returned to the area hoping to set up a mission station.

However, as Krapf was travelling to River Tana, Chief Kivoi was attacked and killed, leaving Krapf in a dilemma. He reached River Tana and ended up there since his guide had been killed already. Krapf translated The New Testament into Swahili and also wrote a Swahili dictionary and grammar.

The reports written by both Dr Ludwig Krapf and Rebmann encouraged the Europeans to come to East Africa in order to look for the source of the Nile. Krapf left East Africa in 1853 owing to ill-health. By that time, the impact of the missionary work of both Krapf and Rebmann was insignificant. As Colonel Playfair found out when he visited Rabai in 1864, only six people had been baptised and another six were receiving baptism lessons.

Johann Rebmann

Johann Rebmann joined Krapf at Rabai in 1846. He was one of the pioneer missionaries in East Africa. Like his contemporary, Krapf was a German, and a member of the CMS.

He explored the areas around the Taita Hills in 1847 and Chagga, where he met Chief Makinga, in 1848.

Rebmann was the first white man to see Mt Kilimanjaro and its snow-capped peak. He lived in East Africa until 1873 when he had become very old and blind. He had a remarkable influence not only in East Africa but also in Europe. He spread the Gospel uncompromisingly. He was well known as a friendly man who was very close to Chief Makinga.

Rebmann's reports about the snow-capped Kilimanjaro and the inland sea of East Africa (Lake Victoria) provoked European geographical curiosity. They also encouraged many missionaries to come to East Africa.

Ludwig Krapf   **Johann Rebmann**

Jacob Erhardt

Erhardt came to East Africa in 1849 and joined Krapf and Rebmann at Rabai. He was also a German but also a prominent member of the CMS. He was one of the pioneer missionaries in East Africa.

Erhardt met Arabs and Swahili from whom he gathered information about the interior of East Africa. On the basis of some of this information, he drew a very inaccurate map of the interior of East Africa, particularly of the lake systems.

This map further stimulated the geographical curiosity of Europe and many explorers poured into East Africa in order to confirm his impressions. Erhardt, however, failed to establish any mission station in the interior of East Africa. Nevertheless, other missionaries continued to spearhead the founding of stations in the interior despite the tropical diseases which killed some of them and slowed down the progress of their work.

Travellers or explorers in East Africa

For about two thousand years, the mystery of the source of the Nile remained unsolved, a fact that embarrassed many geographers in Europe. At the end of the 18th century, James Bruce, a Scotsman, traced the Blue Nile to its source in Ethiopia. The main Nile and its possible connection to the Congo river system remained a mystery. Two British soldiers, Richard Burton and John Hannington Speke, volunteered to come to East Africa and try to solve part of the mystery.

Burton and Speke

Both Burton and Speke were very adventurous British soldiers. They were sent by the Royal Geographical Society in 1856 to look for the source of the Nile. They arrived in Zanzibar in 1856 and prepared for their task. In 1857, they set off along the Arab trade route from Bagamoyo to Kazeh where they learnt of the existence of lakes.

The two explorers were generally sickly. Speke had eye problems while Burton suffered from fever; this made them move very slowly. It took them eight months to reach Lake Tanganyika. They ran short of supplies and they also had a very poor relationship with the Arabs and Africans at Ujiji. Their expedition was not actually supported by these Arabs and Africans.

However, they managed to explore part of the lake, and probably they obtained information from the local people that there was no river connecting Lake Tanganyika with the Nile. Since they did not enjoy any support among the local people, and since they now had no supplies left, they had no alternative but to go back the way they had come.

Speke left Burton at Kazeh and proceeded northwards. He reached Mwanza and after seeing the lake, he named it Lake Victoria after the Queen of England. Although Speke claimed that this lake was the source of the Nile, he had no concrete proof and when he returned to Kazeh, Burton did not believe that the lake was really the source of the Nile. As a result, there was an argument between the two men which nearly made them enemies. Both of them afterwards returned to England.

In England, Speke speedily organised a new expedition to come back and confirm his claim. He got support from the British government and the Royal Geographical Society.

Accompanied by his friend, James Grant, Speke led a caravan of about 217 people back into the interior of East Africa in 1860. This time, as they travelled along the slave route to Kazeh, they became involved in many wars between the Arabs and the Africans, and were attacked by suspicious people and chiefs. But Speke and his people received a cordial welcome in the Karagwe kingdom from King Rumanika.

In January 1862, Speke travelled northwards to Buganda. His friend, Grant, was sick so he was left behind with Rumanika in Karagwe. At that time, the Kabaka of Buganda was Mutesa I, about whose powerful kingdom Speke had already heard. Speke met with a very warm and cordial welcome and was treated well.

Grant joined Speke in Buganda in May. When they wanted to proceed on their journey, the Kabaka was not quite ready to release them because they had requested permission to pass through the territory of his enemy, King Kamurasi of Bunyoro. They were only granted permission to leave the kingdom in July 1862. They became the first Europeans to see the source of the Nile and named the falls 'Ripon', after the then President of the Royal Geographical Society. Thus, Speke solved the mystery of the Nile which had puzzled the Europeans for more than two thousand years.

Speke and Grant then followed the Nile through Bunyoro and Sudan and they met Sir Samuel Baker in the same year. Sir Samuel Baker was an explorer who was also eager to

Kabaka Mutesa meets Speke and Stanley

discover the source of Nile. Speke and Grant reached Khartoum in April 1863.

From there Speke sent a report to Britain saying that the mystery of the Nile had been solved.

Sir Samuel Baker
Baker and his wife wanted to trace the Nile from its mouth to its source, but they were overtaken by Speke's success. However, they still continued, until they reached a lake which they named Lake Albert, after Queen Victoria's husband. They therefore became the first Europeans to see Lake Albert and also the Kabalega falls which they named after Murchison, the president of the Royal Geographical Society at that time. In November 1864, the Bakers started their journey back home. They reached Khartoum in 1865 and finally went back to England.

Dr David Livingstone
Livingstone was a prominent Christian missionary in East Africa who also sought to find the source of the Nile. He made his first missionary journey between 1853 and 1857.

Samuel Baker

After this journey he addressed Cambridge University about the horrors of the slave trade. His speech led to the formation of the Universities Mission to Central Africa (UMCA). David Livingstone was convinced that the presence of European missionary teachers and traders in Africa would lead Africans to a higher level of civilisation, in which Christianity and commerce would flourish.

Like other Europeans, Livingstone did not believe that Speke had truly found the source of the Nile. Accordingly, he was asked by the President of the Royal Geographical Society to go back to Africa to find out the truth. Livingstone started his journey in April 1866 at the mouth of River Ruvuma to the southern end of Lake Malawi and travelled to the northwestern part of the lake, looking for the source of the Nile. In March 1871, Livingstone tried to explore the Lualaba River (tributary of River Congo) but the Arab slave raiders harassed him and he returned to Ujiji in October 1871.

In Europe, a rumour spread that David Livingstone was either dead or lost. So Henry Morton Stanley was sent to Africa by the newspaper he was working for to confirm whether Livingstone was alive or dead. Stanley met Livingstone at Ujiji in 1871 and both of them carefully surveyed the northern shores of Lake Tanganyika. They proved beyond doubt that neither the Nile nor its tributary flowed out of Lake Tanganyika. They went back to Tabora, and there Stanley tried to convince David Livingstone to go back to Europe in vain. Stanley returned to Europe alone on 14 March 1872.

Livingstone still wanted to explore River Lualaba further as he thought that it could easily be a tributary of the Nile. Unfortunately, he died in May 1873 near Lake Bengweulu before he found out the truth. The death of Dr David Livingstone was a turning point in the missionary work in East Africa. It created an urgent need to speed up the struggle to abolish the slave trade and resettle the emancipated slaves.

In 1864 Bishop Tozer and the UMCA came to Zanzibar after an unsuccessful attempt to establish a mission station on Shire mainland. They campaigned vigorously against the slave trade, and for resettlement of the freed slaves. They set up a centre for freed slaves at Bagamoyo in 1868 at which former slaves were taught basic skills such as agriculture and carpentry, as well as reading and writing.

Generally Livingstone's death made him a hero. His body was carried from Chitambo near Lake Bangweulu by his followers up to the coast where it was shipped to Europe and buried among other heroes at Westminster Abbey.

Henry Morton Stanley

buried among other heroes at Westminster Abbey.

Stanley was a journalist by profession. In 1871, as already mentioned, he had come to East Africa to look for David Livingstone who was presumed dead or lost.

Stanley was a very committed explorer and journalist. He came back to East Africa in 1874 to complete the work which was left unfinished by Livingstone. He was a very forceful man who did not allow anything or any person to impede his movement. He set off from Bagamoyo and reached Lake Victoria within 104 days. He travelled all around the lake in a canoe within eight weeks and he proved that Lake Victoria (Nyanza) was really a very large inland sea.

He also visited Buganda Kingdom and met Kabaka Mutesa. He was highly impressed by the power of Buganda. Mutesa gave him a very cordial welcome because he wanted allies against his local enemies as well as against the Egyptian imperialists who were proving to be a big threat to his kingdom. He also invited the Christian missionaries to come and convert his people. He went back to Ujiji where he made friends with both Mirambo and Rumanika.

Penetration of the interior of East Africa from Egypt

Mutesa, the Kabaka of Buganda, was worried about the expansionist policies of the Khedive. Khedive Ismail was the ruler of Egypt. He was so ambitious that he wanted to extend his empire as far south as Lake Victoria. He therefore sent out his agents to extend his political influence in the interior of East Africa, especially present-day Uganda. In 1872, Baker was sent to Uganda and he clashed with Kabalega of Bunyoro, burning Kabalega's capital to ashes. Mutesa viewed the attack on Kabalega's capital as something that was likely to befall his

In 1874 Khedive Ismail sent Charles Gordon to meet Mutesa and declare Egyptian supremacy over Buganda. Gordon instead sent Chaille-Long as his own envoy to Buganda. Chaille-Long became the third European to arrive in Buganda. Ironically, Chaille-Long went back and claimed that he had already annexed Buganda and diverted all the ivory trade from Zanzibar to Gondokoro. This made the Khedive happy and he responded by sending Linant de Bellefonds who arrived in Buganda on 5 April 1875, four days before HM Stanley.

Since Mutesa had executed some 200 Muslims for disobeying his order to eat meat slaughtered by non-Muslims, he feared that the Egyptians, who were Muslims, would avenge the death of their fellow Muslims. Furthermore, the interpreter of one of Mutesa's dreams had said that there was a very serious danger from the north, probably posed by the Egyptians. The apparent threat by the Egyptians induced Mutesa to readily welcome HM Stanley and to invite European missionaries to Buganda.

Problems of explorers

- During their journeys, the explorers covered very long distances on foot. For instance, it took Speke and Burton eight months to travel from Bagamoyo to Lake Tanganyika.

- Tropical diseases, especially malaria, afflicted them. For example, when Speke travelled north from Tabora, he left Burton behind because Burton was attacked by fever. Speke also had an eye problem.

- The explorers met very stiff opposition from the Arabs and some African leaders, especially at Ujiji as well as in Buganda.

- They could not communicate to their homes easily due to lack of means of communication.

- They also had difficulty communicating with the local people because they did not know the local languages. This often led to misunderstandings, conflicts and even wars between Africans and the European explorers.

wars between Africans and the European explorers.
- Disagreements between the explorers slowed down their work. For instance, the disagreement between Speke and Burton was a setback in the search for the source of the Nile.
- Usually the explorers were short of supplies and it was always very hard to replenish them owing to the distance from the coast.

Christian missionaries in Buganda

Stanley was deeply impressed by Kabaka Mutesa and he wrote a letter to London to invite the missionaries to come to Buganda. He sent Linant de Bellefonds to deliver it. Although de Bellefonds was killed in southern Sudan, the letter was found in his boot and sent to England. The *Daily Telegraph* published the letter and the missionaries were offered plenty of funds for their work in Buganda.

The first Protestant missionaries were sent out in 1875. These were a group of about eight people, including Shergold Smith, O'Neil, and Rev. C.T. Wilson. They arrived in Buganda in 1877 and were received warmly by Kabaka Mutesa I. A.M. Mackay joined them in 1878.

In 1879, the Roman Catholic White Fathers established their stations at Tabora and Kibanga as well as at Rubaga as part of their carefully planned advance into East Africa. The White Fathers' 1879 group comprised Father

Kabaka Mutesa I

By 1880, there were four important religions in Buganda: Protestant, Roman Catholic, Islam and traditional. Missionary work in Buganda was successful and many people, including the leaders, were converted to Christianity. Religious conflicts soon developed among the different faiths.

Why missionary work thrived in Uganda

- The Kiganda traditional religion did not have any powerful leaders, therefore it could not resist the influence of Christianity. As a result many Baganda abandoned their religions for the new religion. At the time Christianity came to Buganda, the *Lubaale* cults had been under the control of the Kabaka who was not divine and could not defend the cults. So there was nobody to defend the traditional religions. Furthermore, many Baganda converted to Christianity in order to appease their Kabaka or win favours and rewards from him.

- The Europeans who came to Buganda were great teachers and educationists. The Baganda therefore rated the white man highly and they believed that by embracing the religion of the white man, they would also acquire his knowledge.

- The conversion of the chiefs in Buganda was largely due to their daily contacts with the missionaries. The chiefs influenced their subjects also to be converted.

- The Baganda were receptive to new ideas. That is why they accepted Christianity readily.

- Mutesa wanted to establish a strong centralised religious authority so as to counteract the influence of the traditional gods which still had their powers linked to the Bataka.

Much as the Christian missionaries were successful in their work in Buganda, they did not succeed in converting Kabaka Mutesa to Christianity for the following reasons:-

- When Mutesa organised a reception for the White Fathers, Father Lourdel appealed to Mackay to explain why they had come to Buganda. This was the beginning of a serious discord between the Protestants and the Roman Catholics.

- The two missionary groups did not give the Kabaka the firearms which he had expected from them.

- The Kabaka's advisers told him not to get converted to either of the Christian faiths, i.e. Protestantism and Catholicism.

- The CMS had started stopping the mediums of the Baganda gods from entering the court, which did not please the Kabaka. Some of the Christian missionaries were insincere. They made promises to Mutesa that they did not fulfil. They therefore gave the impression of being people who were unprincipled and disrespectful to the Kabaka.

To make matters worse, the new religions had made his subjects, especially the pages, disrespectful to the Kabaka. These subjects were more loyal to the missionaries than their Kabaka, an offence punishable by death in Buganda.

The relationship between Mwanga and the missionaries

Mwanga ascended the throne after the death of his father, Mutesa I, in 1884. He was only 18 years old. Unlike his predecessors, such as Kabaka Suna and Mutesa, Mwanga was erratic and undiplomatic in his handling of issues in Buganda. He failed to establish royal leadership. He always sought advice on how to run the kingdom from his agemates at the court.

Mwanga was not on good terms with the old chiefs in his kingdom. They played upon his fears when the Germans occupied Tanganyika. They told him that the missionaries represented the spearhead of European imperialism. His fears were made worse when the Arabs warned him about European imperialism. Mwanga's reaction was furious. He ordered his subjects not to associate with the missionaries. When the subjects defied his order, Mwanga asserted his royal authority by executing three converts of the Church Missionary Society in January 1885.

In November of the same year, Mwanga ordered the death of Hannington, the first CMS bishop in Uganda. He had been made to believe that those who would usurp his power would come from the East. In June 1886, at Namugongo, Mwanga put to death thirty Christian converts who had refused to renounce their faith. These are the ones referred to as the Uganda Martyrs and who are remembered annually on June 3rd.

However, by 1888, Christians and Muslims in Buganda could no longer tolerate the persecution, so they combined and deposed Mwanga. He fled south of Lake Victoria and was replaced by his brother, Kiwewa. Kiwewa was in turn deposed by the Muslims because he had refused to be circumcised. He had also, together with his chiefs, refused to comply with the demands of the Islamic religion. He was replaced by Kalema.

In 1888, the Christians supported Mwanga to fight the Muslims, and in October of the same year, Kalema was deposed along with all his Muslim supporters. Shortly after re-enthronement of Mwanga, quarrels erupted between the Protestants and the Catholics. Things came to a head in 1892 when the two groups disagreed on power-sharing in the Lukiiko. This disagreement caused problems for the Christian missionaries. In addition to the quarrel over power-sharing, there existed another problem: Mwanga was accused of yielding to undue pressure from Protestants when he released a Protestant that had murdered a Catholic.

War erupted between the two missionary groups in January 1892. Mwanga supported the Catholics while the Protestants were supported by Captain Lugard, the representative of the IBEA company. The Protestants won the war because they had superior weapons and also the support of a well trained and well organised force led by Lugard. The persecution of the Christians by Mwanga and the several attacks on the missionaries by the Muslims prompted the missionaries to request British intervention. This eventually led to the colonisation of Uganda.

Ex-king Mwanga (right) in custody (1899)

The results of missionary work in East Africa
Negative results
- Buganda became the springboard for Christianity to spread to all parts of Uganda.

- Christianity led to the decay of traditional religion since traditional religion, according to Christian teaching, is associated with paganism, witchcraft and satanic activities.

- Christianity led to the death of many Baganda, including Christian converts at Namugongo who were burnt alive in June 1886.

- Christianity divided the Baganda into *Wa-Ingereza* and *Wa-Faransa* during the Mengo battle.

- Christianity led to the formation of religious political parties in the 1950s and 60s.

- The missionaries undermined the Africans' confidence in their culture which was denounced as satanic, and became agents of European cultural imperialism.

Positive results

- Medical centres were established as a result of missionary work in Buganda; for instance at Mengo, Nsambya and Rubaga. These hospitals helped to reduce the death rate in Buganda.

- Many primary schools were built to encourage formal education; for instance, Buddo and Gayaza. Meanwhile, in other parts of East Africa, schools were also built in order to spread Western education.

- They established institutions such as seminaries. In 1893 the first seminary was opened and just after ten years, i.e. 1913, the first Catholic priest graduated from the seminary.

- The missionaries contributed immensely to the creation of the first African elite which included people such as Stanislaus Mugwanya and Apolo Kaggwa who became renowned leaders in Buganda.

- They facilitated the signing of the Buganda Agreement of 1900 by acting as intermediaries between the British colonialists and the Baganda chiefs.

- The missionaries fought the slave trade and also looked after the freed slaves.

- They taught East Africans to read and write in their mother tongues. The missionaries set up printing presses to print books translated into indigenous languages. Foreign languages taught by the missionaries became very important during the time when Africans were agitating for their independence. Africans were able to express themselves to their colonial masters in English, Kiswahili, French, etc.

- The missionaries introduced cash crops and set up experimental stations. They also introduced new methods of producing commodities for export.

- The missionaries encouraged legitimate trade which replaced the slave trade.

Revision 14

1   (a)   Describe the problems faced by Christian missionaries in East Africa during the second half of the 19th century.

     (b)   What impact did their activities have on the peoples of East Africa?

2   (a)   What were the *Wa-Faransa* and *Wa-Ingereza* wars in Uganda?

     (b)   What were the effects of these wars on the people of Uganda up to 1962?

3   (a)   Why were the Christian missionaries interested in East Africa?

     (b)   What were the results of their activities?

4   (a)   Why did the Christian missionaries come to East Africa?

     (b)   What problems did they face in the course of establishing themselves in East Africa?

15

European traders in East Africa

After the transfer of his capital from Oman to Zanzibar, Sayyid Said promoted trade at the East African coast by attracting many Europeans to his empire. By 1844, he had signed commercial treaties with the United States of America, Britain, Belgium, Austria and Hungary. He had also accepted British and American consuls in 1837 and 1841, respectively.

In the early part of the 19th century, international trade was limited to the coast. The main exports were ivory, gum, copal, cloves, copra and skins. The imports included cloth, spirits, beads and glass. The European traders agitated for the abolition of slave trade and the introduction of legitimate trade in the hope that this would promote the market for their goods and provide essential raw materials.

Trading companies in East Africa

Through their reports on the situation in East Africa, the missionaries and explorers played a great role in convincing the traders to come to East Africa. Most of the trading companies were very hesitant to come to East Africa for two important reasons. Unlike in West Africa where there were navigable rivers, there was none in East Africa. The traders were not ready to construct roads or railways since they were not certain of the existence of valuable raw materials that would help recover their money. Secondly, the traders did not expect to find minerals in East Africa.

The Livingstone Central Africa Trading Company was founded in 1878 by James Stevenson, a Scottish businessman. Its initial aim was to establish trading posts between Lake Malawi and Lake Tanganyika and to supply goods to maintain the missionaries. The company also wanted to discourage slave trade and to promote legitimate trade. Its other projects included a steamer service on Lake Malawi, a steamer operating on Lake Tanganyika for the London Missionary Society and the building of Stevenson Road joining Lakes Nyasa and Tanganyika. At this time also, there was increasing competition among the European traders along the East Africa coast. In order to curtail this competition, France and Germany were denied trading concessions as a result of pressure from John Kirk, the British consul, on the Sultan of Zanzibar.

William Mackinnon and IBEA Co.

William Mackinnon was the most outstanding and most active European trader in East Africa. He started a steamship service round the Indian coast in 1856 and his business prospered. He named his company the British India Steam Navigation Company. His ships began calling at the coast of East Africa.

Mackinnon became a friend to Sayyid Majid and he encouraged him to develop Dar-es-Salaam. He was given the go-ahead to build a road from Dar-es-Salaam to Lake Malawi. He set up a mail service in Zanzibar in 1872. This greatly improved communication with Europe.

Sayyid Barghash, whom William befriended, succeeded Sayyid Majid. Mackinnon convinced Barghash to lease the whole of the mainland from Tanga to Waisheik with its entire hinterland, an area of 1,528,000 square kilometres, for fifty years to a company which he would form. The project was a failure because there was no single European investor who was willing to risk his capital despite the interest which was shown by the missionaries. The project was not supported by the British government.

Mackinnon formed the British East African Association in 1887. This association aimed at trading in the mainland territories of the Sultan of Zanzibar. Sultan Barghash granted the association judicial and political powers and the right to levy customs on the mainland between Kapini and Umba River for fifty years. In 1888, the authority of the association was extended 300 kilometres inland from the coast.

On 3rd September, the British company won recognition from Britain and it was granted a royal charter under the name of the Imperial British East African Company (IBEA Co).

The relationship between IBEA Co. and other companies at the East African coast

The IBEA Co. was given a charter in the hope that it would lead to the development of trade within the British sphere of influence. Secondly, it was entrusted with the task of overseeing British interests in its sphere of influence in East Africa based on the Anglo-German Agreement of 1886. Karl Peters had already started a company in 1884 which became German East African Company. The rise of IBEA Co. and the German East African Company aroused mutual fears in Britain and Germany about the respective intentions of each country in East Africa especially with regard to Uganda.

Because of the rivalry between IBEA Co. and the German company, an agreement was concluded in 1890. This was called the Anglo-German Agreement or the Heligoland Treaty under which the Germans recognised Uganda as being within the British sphere of influence. In December of the same year, IBEA Co sent its first representative to Uganda. This was Captain Frederick Lugard. Lugard concluded a treaty with Buganda giving IBEA Co. some political rights in the kingdom in 1892.

German East Africa Company (GEA Co.)

This company was founded by Karl Peters for the German Colonisation Society in 1884. The following year it was granted a charter by the German emperor to safeguard German interests in East Africa. The company signed treaties with chiefs in the Usambara and Kilimanjaro areas. All these treaties were presented at the Berlin Conference of 1885 and this helped the German government to acquire Wangara, Ungulu, Ukami, Uzigua, Kilimanjaro and Witu. Germany also obtained access to Dar-es-Salaam.

Problems faced by the trading companies

- They met a great deal of opposition from African leaders.

- Lack of support from their home governments. For instance, when the IBEA Co. proposed to lease the mainland of East Africa, the British government did not give him any support.

- Poor transport and communication. There were no roads, no railway lines, etc. so traders had to walk, sometimes over very long distances.

- Rivalry between the companies. For instance, the rivalry between IBEA Co. and GEA Co. at the coast and in Uganda was fierce.

- The companies also had very little financial backing. This frustrated their ambitious trading plans from time to time.

- They had a shortage of qualified manpower. Most of the employees working in the company were not qualified for their jobs. This adversely affected the performance of the companies.

Impact of trading companies in East Africa

The presence of trading companies led to the systematic European colonisation of East Africa. Some of the agreements made at their initiative put East African countries effectively under the control of rival European powers. For instance, the Anglo-German Agreement of 1886 put Uganda and Kenya under British rule and Tanganyika under German rule. The companies pioneered the development of roads and railways. A good example is the building of the Uganda Railway which was started by IBEA Co. After construction of the Uganda Railway was completed, exploitation of the resources of Kenya and Uganda became possible. The companies also contributed to the improvement of transport and communications. They opened up East Africa to European culture and trade.

Imperialists

An imperialist is a person who believes that his country is the best and that it should rule over other countries either through the use of military force or through diplomacy.

In the 19th century, in East Africa, there were two outstanding European imperialists, namely HH Johnson and Karl Peters.

H.H. Johnston

Johnston was a small, forceful and active Englishman. He had served at Oil Rivers and Cameroon as vice consul; he had also been a commissioner in Central Africa and Malawi. He arrived in Zanzibar in April 1884 to lead a scientific mission to Mount Kilimanjaro. In Zanzibar, he met John Kirk, the British consul, and they became friends. He held the view that his government's rule would improve the situation in East Africa if it was extended to the interior.

Kirk persuaded the Sultan of Zanzibar to allow the extension of British rule to the interior, but Johnston still believed that British rule was suitable for the whole of Africa. He crossed to the mainland and established his base at Moshi.

In Moshi, he made friends with the local chief of the Chagga, Mandara. Chief Mandara thought that Johnston should help him in his conflicts with other Chagga states. Johnston gave a lot of gifts to Mandara, but later they came to mistrust each other and Johnston was forced to move to Taveta. He signed a treaty with the chiefs of Taveta on 27th September 1884, which treaty granted him a 13km² piece of land on which he meant to grow wheat.

In 1899, Johnston was appointed a Special Commissioner in Uganda. He was also entrusted with the duty of reducing Uganda's financial dependence on Britain. Uganda as a British protectorate was becoming a burden to the British taxpayer. Johnston was the chief representative of the British government in negotiations that led to the 1900 Buganda Agreement.

Karl Peters

Karl Peters was a forceful and aggressive German. He arrived in Zanzibar in November 1884 with two other friends. They disguised themselves as mechanics, but they were in fact imperialists. They were impatient with the slow pace at which their home government was acquiring territories in Africa. They formed an association called the German Colonisation Society whose mission was to acquire colonies in Africa for Germany. They moved into the mainland of East Africa and quickly concluded treaties with Usagora, Ungulu, Uzingua and Ukami. All these territories were between rivers Pangani and Rufiji. When they reported the signing of those treaties back home, the German government declared that area part of the German sphere of administration.

The approval of those treaties soon led to the partition of East Africa. After the acquisition of these territories, the German Colonisation Society was given a charter under which the German East African Company was empowered to govern. Karl Peters was appointed to head the company. His overrriding ambition was to get rid of British influence in East Africa. He feared that if the IBEA Co. teamed up with Cecil Rhodes of South Africa, it would spell disaster for the German interests in East Africa. He therefore used the German naval squadron to force the Sultan of Zanzibar to recognise German influence on the mainland, including Witu in the northern part of the East African coast.

The Sultan had no alternative but to agree to the terms of the Germans, and he even reluctantly accepted that the Germans appoint a commission of enquiry. The outcome of this enquiry was that it marginalised the Sultan of Zanzibar by reducing the area of his influence to a mere 16 kilometres inland.

In 1886, Karl Peters directed his efforts towards Uganda. He reached Mwanga's court early in 1890 and secured a treaty from him. Under the treaty, Buganda was to be placed under German rule. Unfortunately, his treaty was overtaken by the Heligoland Treaty of 1890 which recognised Uganda as part of the British sphere of influence.

Karl Peters was appointed a district officer. He, however, treated the African people very cruelly. Allegations against him were investigated and, in 1896, he was tried, found guilty and dismissed from office.

Revision 15

1   (a)   Describe the role played by charter companies in the colonisation of East Africa.

    (b)   What problems did these companies face in East Africa?

2   Describe the activities of the chartered companies in East Africa on the eve of colonisation.

3   Write some short notes on the following:-

    (a)   Karl Peters

    (b)   H.H. Johnston

    (c)   William Makinnon

16

The scramble for and partition of East Africa

Egyptian imperialism

By the mid 19th century, the Egyptians had imperialistic designs on East Africa. They wanted to control the Nile valley from its source to the Mediterranean Sea. They also wanted to control the White Nile, as well as the trade in slaves and ivory along the Nile valley. The Egyptians wanted to recruit slaves into their army. But in the later part of the 19th century, they wanted to appease the Europeans by stopping the slave trade. Another very important reason for their interest in East Africa was their wish to exploit the natural resources of the region.

Sir Samuel Baker's efforts to extend Egyptian rule to Uganda

Baker was a British national who was appointed in 1869 by Khedive Ismail to bring northern Uganda and the interlacustrine region under Egyptian rule. These areas were referred to as 'Equatorial Province'. Samuel Baker was also expected to take part in efforts to abolish the slave trade. Another task which he had to accomplish was to extend Egyptian influence in Equatorial Province. By 1872, Baker had arrived in Bunyoro and met the Omukama Kabalega in Masindi. He pronounced that from that time onwards, Bunyoro would be under Egyptian rule.

Baker had, however, underestimated Kabalega's resolve to resist foreign domination. In June 1872, just two months after Baker's pronouncement, Kabalega declared war against the Egyptian agent.

126

Omukama Kabalega

Though Kabalega was defeated and his capital burnt down, he continued launching guerrilla attacks on Baker who had to retreat from Masindi to Fomena. Baker sided with Rionga, Kabalega's rival. He established his headquarters at Patiko, from where he frequently sent out expeditions against Kabalega.

However, Baker did not achieve his objectives. Consequently, he abandoned his plans and went back to London in 1873, never to come back. He left behind a garrison of soldiers commanded by an Egyptian.

Charles Gordon

Gordon was an Englishman who succeeded Sir Samuel Baker as governor of Equatorial Province in 1873. His role was similar to that of his predecessor. He was supposed to annex Buganda for Egypt and also to abolish the slave trade. In order to accomplish his missions, Gordon established his headquarters at Patiko and persuaded Acholi chiefs to work with him.

In 1874, Gordon received Mutesa's envoys who had been sent to seek peace and alliance with Egypt. Unfortunately, Gordon thought that Mutesa had already accepted Egyptian rule. Later on, Gordon sent Chaille-Long to annex Buganda for Egypt. Chaille-Long, deceived by the apparent friendliness of Mutesa, went back and claimed that Buganda had been annexed, and then diverted the ivory trade from Zanzibar to Egypt.

Matters came to a head when Gordon sent Linant de Bellefonds with seventy indisciplined soldiers to Buganda. They were attacked before they reached Buganda at Namuyonjo, which was a vassal state of Bunyoro. Gordon then sent Nuer Agar with 150 soldiers to try and annex Buganda. All Gordon's soldiers were disarmed and imprisoned by Mutesa I. Gordon persuaded the Khedive to try to invade Buganda from the Indian Ocean, but this did not materialise. Therefore, Gordon had to accept the independence of Buganda.

Importance of Egyptian imperialism in East Africa

- Khedive Ismail's goal of stopping the slave trade was a pretext to gain influence up the Nile valley.

- Egyptian imperialism was a threat to the independence of the peoples and a forerunner of foreign control and domination.

- The Egyptians challenged British policy towards Zanzibar.

- The Egyptians involved the British more and more in the affairs of East Africa.

- Egyptian imperialism indirectly paved the way for British occupation of Uganda.

The European scramble for and partition of East Africa (1884 - 1900)

To 'scramble' means to rush and compete for something with other people in order to get a share of it. 'Partition' means carving up. In our case, it means the division of East Africa between the British and the Germans.

Reasons for the scramble and partition

- By 1880, industrialised European countries needed markets for their surplus goods outside Europe. So they acquired colonies to ensure that they were not excluded from Africa by their rivals.

- The Europeans partitioned Africa in order to obtain raw materials like coffee and cotton for their home industries.

- The European nations partitioned Africa in order to invest their surplus capital.

- The European powers wanted to resettle in Africa.

- Some of the Europeans wanted to abolish the slave trade. This could only be done through the surplus population.

- The newly created state of Germany wanted to gain prestige by colonising East Africa and other parts of Africa.

- The missionaries exerted pressure on their home governments to take over East Africa in order to create favourable conditions for the spread of Christianity.

- The reports of the explorers on climate, fertility of the land, etc. facilitated the scramble for, and partition of, East Africa.

- The immediate cause of the scramble for East Africa was the activities of King Leopold II of Belgium in Congo. He formed an association purportedly to abolish the slave trade yet he wanted to acquire territory. So the British and Germans moved into East Africa partly to pre-empt his expansionist ambitions.

- Jingoism or fanatical nationalism also caused the scramble for East Africa. To most of the Europeans, having a vast empire or possession of colonies was a symbol of greatness.

- The shift in the balance of power in Europe, especially after the unification of Germany and Italy, stimulated the scramble for Africa.

The Berlin Conference

In the 1880s there were widespread fears that the unregulated rush for colonies in Africa by the European powers could lead to war in Europe. Accordingly, Bismarck, the German Chancellor, convened the Berlin Conference in November 1884 to draw up the ground rules for the partition of Africa. This conference went on up to February 1885.

Terms of the Berlin Conference

i) The protectorate claimed by any power would not be recognised unless there was effective occupation of that protectorate by the power claiming it.

ii) Slave trade had to be stopped wherever it existed in Africa.

iii) The Congo basin was open to all European traders and Europeans were not encouraged to fight fellow Europeans but Africans.

iv) Togoland, the Cameroons and South-West Africa were recognised as German territories.

v) The British claim to Niger was recognised and all the Delta region became their protectorate.

vi) Leopold II's claim to the Congo basin was also recognised.

The process of partition

By 1990 the whole of East Africa had been partitioned. As already mentioned, Britain and Germany reached an agreement in 1886 under which the area between the Tana and Ruvuma rivers was divided by a straight line running from Umba River to Lake Victoria. The northern part became a British sphere of influence while the Germans took over the southern part. In fact, this line became the Tanzania - Kenya border of today.

On 24 March 1887, William Mackinnon, president of the British East African Association, leased a sixteen kilometre coastal stretch between River Umba and Kipini for fifty years and he was granted a charter.

The Anglo-German Agreement of 1886 did not include Uganda. Rivalry between Germany and Britain became serious because Buganda was very important to Britain strategically since the Nile is the lifeblood of Egypt, then a British colony. This rivalry was resolved by the Heligoland Treaty of 1890 under which the Germans recognised Uganda as part of the British sphere of influence in exchange for Heligoland in the North Sea. Germany also abandoned Witu, Zanzibar and Pemba which together became a British protectorate. Germany also bought the tract of land which had been leased by Mackinnon. The Uganda - Tanzania border extended westwards 1°S to the Congo border.

Revision 16

1   (a)   Why were Europeans interested in East Africa in the 19th century?

(b)   What roles did the Imperial East Africa Company and the German East Africa Company play in the colonization of East Africa?

2   Describe the role of the following in the colonisation of East Africa:-

(a)   Frederick Lugard

(b)   Karl Peters.

3   (a)   Which European countries were involved in the scramble for East Africa?

(b)   Why were they interested in the colonisation of East Africa?

4   (a)   Why did Europeans show a growing interest in East Africa between 1775 and 1875?

(b)   Describe European activity in East Africa during this period.

5   Using examples, show how the activities of the following European groups led to the scramble for East Africa:-

(a)   Explorers and traders

(b)   Missionaries

6 (a)   Why were different European countries interested in East Africa in the 19th century?

(b)   What role did the charter companies play in the colonisation of East Africa?

17

British conquest and occupation of Uganda (1884 - 1914)

The British had a number of interests in Uganda. First and foremost, they wanted to spread Christianity. Secondly, at that time Britain had already declared the slave trade illegal in Britain and in her territories, so they intended to stop the inhuman slave trade. They also took into account Uganda's fertile soils and good climate which were very suitable for investment of the surplus capital obtained from the products of their industries. Furthermore, they wanted to obtain new materials for their industries. They also wanted to create a captive market for goods in Uganda.

Uganda was strategically positioned as the source of the Nile. The British wanted to colonise it in order to safeguard their interests in Egypt, especially the shortest sea route to India via the Suez Canal. If any other European power acquired Uganda, it could jeopardise the British interests in Egypt by simply diverting the Nile.

Captain Lugard and Buganda

Once the Heligoland Treaty of 1890 was signed, the IBEA concentrated on extending its influence in Uganda. In 1890, Frederick Lugard arrived in Buganda as the first IBEA Co. agent. He forced Mwanga to sign a treaty accepting British rule on 26 December 1890. The terms of this treaty were as follows:

(i) Lugard was to be resident at the Kabaka's court and have authority over all the white men.

(ii) The supply of arms was to be regulated and only people with licences were to be permitted to own guns.

(iii) Lugard was to be in charge of the principal state officials of Buganda who had control over the collection of revenue in the kingdom.

(iv) There was to be religious tolerance between the white missionaries and other religious groups in Buganda.

(v) Lugard was to settle any disputes between missions.

Captain F. Lugard

Buganda therefore became Captain Frederick Lugard's base to extend the company's rule in Uganda.

In 1891, Lugard was joined by Captain Williams. Immediately, Lugard led an army to the Buganda - Bunyoro border against the Baganda Muslim refugees. Having defeated them, he returned to Mwanga's capital. Later he departed for western Uganda, leaving Captain Williams behind in Buganda.

Lugard's expedition in western Uganda

On his way to western Uganda, Lugard met Kasagama, the young ruler of Toro, who had just been deposed by Kabalega of Bunyoro. When Lugard reached Nkore, he met the son of King Ntare V. The prince established a blood relationship with Lugard and accepted the company's flag as a symbol of British rule over Nkore. Ntare further promised Lugard that the trade in guns would be stopped and Lugard gave him a gift of cloth in return. Nkore became a British protectorate.

Emin Pasha

Lugard proceeded to Toro and reinstated Kasagama. In appreciation, Kasagama signed a treaty accepting British protection. He also promised to stop trade in arms across his country, to give ivory to the IBEA Co. and also to stop the slave trade. He went on to recruit the redundant Sudanese soldiers left behind by Emin Pasha into his army.

Lugard's achievements in western Uganda

Kasagama

He was successful in bringing Nkore and Toro under IBEA Co. rule.

His actions in western Uganda also brought to an end the destructive sale of arms from Tanzania to Kabalega of Bunyoro. He was also successful in reinstating Kasagama. Lugard also stopped the slave trade through his treaties with Nkore and Toro. Furthermore, he re-engaged soldiers who had been abandoned by Emin Pasha.

Lugard returns to Buganda

Lugard's success in western Uganda strengthened his influence in Buganda. However, upon his return from his expedition in western Uganda, Lugard found a letter from the IBEA Co. saying that the company was closing down because it had become bankrupt. In order to forestall Lugard's imminent departure from Uganda, the CMS donated $40,000 to keep the company running until the end of 1892.

Fighting soon broke out between the Protestants and Catholics, and Mwanga supported the Catholics while Lugard supported the Protestants. As we have already seen, the Protestants won the war. Mwanga and his supporters were driven out of the kingdom, but shortly afterwards he was allowed to return under a new agreement signed on 5th April 1892. The terms of the agreement were as follows:

(i) Mwanga would accept British protection in totality.

(ii) He would never declare war without the consent of the British Resident.

(iii) The IBEA Co. would recognise the power of the Kabaka.

(iv) All arms and the slave trade would be officially abolished.

(v) All the Europeans in Buganda would be under the control of the IBEA Co.

Mbogo, a Muslim leader who was in Bunyoro with his supporters, came back and endorsed the agreement on behalf of his followers.

Uganda was directly taken over by the British government in 1894. Financing the administration of Uganda however became very expensive. For instance, between 1897 and 1898 Britain spent £89,000 to administer Uganda. Between 1899 - 1900 Britain spent £397,000. These expenses forced the British government to explore ways of cutting costs. H.H. Johnston was charged with this responsibility.

Buganda Agreement

This was a document signed between Sir Henry Johnston and the Baganda chiefs on behalf of Kabaka Chwa who was still an infant.

Reasons for the signing of Buganda Agreement in 1900

Several reasons were given for the signing of the Buganda Agreement.

- The earlier agreements did not properly define the boundaries of Buganda. So the British wanted this done.

- The British wanted to use the agreement as a springboard for the integration of all other parts of Uganda into what would be called Uganda.

- The British further wanted to know about the natural resources of Buganda and exploit them.

- They wanted to put the economy of their colony on a sound footing.

- They wanted to end the influence of Kabalega of Bunyoro.

- The British were concerned about the expenses which were involved in running the protectorate from Britain using British funds. So they wanted Buganda and Uganda to cover their administrative costs from local sources. These sources would include taxation.

Terms of Buganda Agreement

The negotiations between Sir Henry Johnston and the Baganda leaders took two and a half months and finally an agreement was reached in which the following specific terms were reached. This agreement changed the history of Buganda completely.

1. The boundaries of the kingdom were defined and they encompassed the lost counties of Bugangaizi and Buyaga.

2. The Kabaka and chiefs of Uganda were to renounce in favour of Her Majesty the Queen any claim of tribute on provinces of Uganda.

3. Buganda was to be ranked and treated like any other provinces of Uganda.

4. The revenue of Buganda Kingdom would be merged into the general revenue collected by the administration of Uganda Protectorate.

5. The laws made for the governance of Uganda Protectorate would apply equally to Buganda Kingdom.

6. The Kabaka was to be referred to as His Highness, the Kabaka of Uganda and on his death, his successor was to be elected by the majority of votes in the Lukiiko or Native Council.

- The Kabaka's native court was restricted to act with certain limited powers. For example, the native court was to have no powers to issue a death sentence.

- The Kabaka was to be paid an allowance of £1,500 a year.

- His regents could also be paid a wage.

7. Namasole, the mother of Kabaka Chwa, was to be paid an allowance of £50 a year during her lifetime. This could not be extended to the mothers of other Kabakas.

8. Civil or criminal cases involving the Baganda and people of other regions of Uganda would be handled by the British courts of justice.

9. Buganda Kingdom was divided into twenty counties for purposes of easy administration.

10. The Kabaka was to appoint three people, i.e. Katikiro (Prime Minister), Treasurer and Chief Justice, with the approval of Her Majesty the Queen of England.

11. The structure of the Lukiiko was defined along with the number of people who were to constitute it.

12. A hut tax of three rupees per annum on any house or hut or habitation used as a dwelling place and a gun tax of three rupees were introduced.

13. The Kabaka lost his independent power to conscript people into the army to defend his Kingdom except on the advice of Her Majesty the Queen of England.

14. Road maintenance was to be taken care of by the native county chiefs.

15. More than half of the estimated area of Buganda Kingdom was recognised as crown land.

- The Kabaka, royal family, princes, regents and chiefs were all alloted land according to their ranks. For example, county chiefs were all granted 8 sq miles of land each as private property and 8 sq miles of land each as official estate.

16. The mineral rights belonged to the Protectorate administration. If such mineral is discovered in a private land, ten percent would be paid to the Protectorate government.

Significance of Buganda Agreement

* The agreement gave Buganda a prominent position in the Protectorate in relation to other provinces. This promoted the policy of divide and rule in Uganda.

* The agreement shifted real power from the Kabaka to the Buganda prime minister and other chiefs since the Kabaka could no longer allocate land.

* The Buganda Agreement stipulated that the Kabaka be called "His Highness", which lowered the Kabaka's status in the light of the traditional powers he held.

* The hereditary traditional position of the Kabaka was altered. The appointment of the Kabaka thenceforth had to be approved by the Protectorate government.

* The ordinary people were reduced to tenants at will.

* The agreement also facilitated the system of indirect rule in Buganda because the kingdom was to be governed through its own institutions such as the Lukiiko rather than those of the central government.

* The agreement stunted the development of a national consciousness.

* The Buganda Agreement was used as a basis for other agreements with Ankole, Toro and Bunyoro.

* The agreement created an affluent land-owning class and the landless poor.

- The Kabaka no longer had much authority over his subjects since court cases were handled by the Protectorate government.

- The Buganda Kingdom was regarded as a mere province of Uganda.

Toro Agreement, 1900

After signing the Buganda Agreement, Sir Johnston proceeded to Toro to sign another agreement which was to establish British rule in that kingdom. The Toro Agreement was signed in June 1900.

Terms of agreement

The Omukama was recognised as the leader of the Toro Kingdom. Gun and hut taxes were introduced in the kingdom.

The kingdom was to be incorporated into the Protectorate. The collection of taxes was to be left in the hands of the chiefs, and the Omukama would then hand the tax money over to the Protectorate government. Almost all the land in Toro was declared crown land. Freehold grants of land were given to the Omukama and his leading chiefs. The interests of the chiefs and the Omukama received more attention than those of the peasants. Toro's independence from Bunyoro was recognised by the agreement.

Ankole Agreement of 1901

Unlike in Toro where the Omukama was recognised as the paramount ruler, in Nkore, Johnston was very reluctant to recognise the Omugabe as paramount leader. This was because the Omugabe had very limited powers over his chiefs.

The Ankole Agreement was only signed when the chiefs agreed to recognise the Omugabe as their paramount ruler. The agreement was signed by Wilson on behalf of the British government. The agreement enlarged Nkore by incorporating Buhweju, Igara, Bunyaruguru and Kajara into Ankole.

The extension of British rule to Bunyoro

The Bunyoro Kingdom was one of the most powerful kingdoms in Uganda by 1894. Its ruler was Kabalega. Bunyoro was very hostile to the British imperialists, and had become a haven for the people who were opposed to the British. Earlier on, Bunyoro had fought and driven away Baker, after inflicting heavy casualties on his men.

In January 1894, Colonel Colville, a new British Commissioner, led a loyalist force from Buganda against Bunyoro. This expedition led to the eventual defeat of Kabalega's army. When his soldiers were defeated, Kabalega fled to Lango. The defeat of Kabalega's army had serious effects on Bunyoro and its relationship with the British in Uganda. The first effect was the construction of various forts to completely separate the western part of Bunyoro from the eastern part. Secondly, as a result of the defeat, much of Bunyoro territory was taken over by Toro and Buganda.

The British appointed Baganda agents as chiefs over the Banyoro. This led to the rebellion of 1907, and the Baganda agents were driven to Hoima (district headquarters). The Banyoro appointed their traditional chiefs to rule over them, but the British organised a military force to teach the Banyoro a lesson. The Banyoro were defeated and about fifty of their chiefs were exiled. The British therefore regarded Bunyoro as conquered territory and felt that there was no need to sign an agreement with it. They did not sign an agreement with Bunyoro until 1933.

The extension of colonial rule to eastern Uganda

Whenever mention is made of the extension of British colonial rule to the north-eastern and eastern parts of Uganda, Semei Kakungulu readily comes to mind.

Kakungulu and his activities in north-eastern and eastern Uganda

Kakungulu was a Muganda born in Kooki. He was a skilful elephant hunter, an activity which brought him to the attention of the Kabaka of Buganda. He grew up at the Kabaka's court as a page. His full name was Semei Kakungulu Kwakirenzi.

Kakungulu demonstrated his military skills early and consequently became one of the Buganda generals. He narrowly missed becoming Buganda's prime minister owing to the presence of Apollo Kaggwa and Stanislaus Mugwanya who were better qualified for the post than him.

As a soldier, Kakungulu actively participated in the religious wars which were fought in Buganda. He took part in fighting, and capturing Kabalega and Mwanga at the border of Lango and Teso. He captured them at a place called Kangai in 1899 and took them to Kampala as captives. Between 1894 and 1904 Semei Kakungulu advanced into Lango and Teso and brought the two areas under British control. In the areas he managed to bring under control, he introduced the Kiganda system of government. He divided those areas into *saza* (counties), *gombolola* (sub-counties), and *muluka* (parishes). He appointed Baganda agents in all those counties to help with colonial administration. He established his headquarters at Budaka in Bukedi. He also established forts in all the conquered areas. Kakungulu was nicknamed the 'Kabaka of Bukedi' because he wanted to create his own empire in eastern Uganda. He had a great liking for such titles. Kakungulu recruited local labour to build roads.

However, the British got concerned about his influence in the East. Consequently in 1901, his headquarters at Budaka was taken over by a British officer and Kakungulu was moved to Mbale. In 1903, the British took over the administration of Mbale. After that, they completely took over the administration of eastern Uganda. Nevertheless, they retained the 'Kakungulu model' of administration in eastern Uganda using the Baganda agents as advisers to the local chiefs.

Kakungulu was appointed president of the Busoga Lukiiko in 1906. In that capacity, he helped the British to unite Busoga which was at that time a patchwork of separate chiefdoms. He introduced the Kiganda system of government, and eventually the Basoga princedoms were welded together under one president, one Lukiiko and the British colonial masters.

142

The British became worried about Kakungulu's progress and popularity in Busoga and planned to get rid of him, especially after they had used him to establish themselves. Kakungulu was transferred to Bukedi in 1913. Kakungulu became disillusioned with the British when they turned against him. As a result, he got involved with a religious sect, the *Abamalaki*, which rejected missionary teachings and Western medicine and urged a return to the ways of the past. This made him lose the respect that he had enjoyed.

Semei Kakungulu

Conflict between Semei Kakungulu and the British

Several reasons were responsible for the conflict between Semei Kakungulu and the British administration. Many Baganda moved into eastern Uganda in the hope of acquiring free land. This meant that there would be fewer people to tax in Buganda, something which the British, who wanted money to run their protectorate, were not happy about. Kakungulu did not stop the Baganda from migrating to the East. Instead he opened an avenue for poor Baganda to acquire land in eastern Uganda. This annoyed both the Lukiiko and the British colonial masters.

The Baganda agents who were appointed to administer eastern Uganda were misbehaving. The result was that in 1901, Walker, a British official, was sent there to find out the truth. He found out that the Baganda agents were involved in extortion of goats, sheep and other property from the peasants. They were also taxing the peasants heavily and the poor people like the Jopadhola could not pay. The British were very angry with the agents.

The extension of Kakungulu's influence in the mountain areas of Bugisu also brought him into conflict with the British.

He allowed himself a lot of land to the dismay of the local people. He also failed to collect hut and gun tax from his followers and his subordinates. When this was reported to the central government, Kakungulu was removed from Budaka and replaced by Walter.

However, Kakungulu went and established himself in Mbale in 1902 where he created an orderly administration. He vigorously promoted the cultivation of bananas. His peaceful administration also attracted Asian traders. He was appointed chief of Mbale County, but he was always closely supervised by the new District Commissioner.

When Kakungulu got fed up with the actions of his District Commissioner, he complained to the higher authorities at Entebbe. Fortunately, his complaints coincided with the arrival of Sir Hesketh Bell as the new Governor of Uganda. The new governor posted him to Busoga. His followers had got into trouble in Bukedi when one of them took some goats and cattle by force, and also seized the wife of a local notable for denying him beer. In protest, the people of Tororo invaded the local headquarters of the Baganda agents and killed everyone they found there.

In Busoga, Semei Kakungulu had hoped to become Kabaka, but he did not succeed in this ambition. The local chiefs resented him and he was transferred back to Bukedi. He died an unhappy man in 1929.

Extension of colonial rule in northern Uganda

For a long time, the northern part of Uganda was regarded as not very useful since the British knew little about it by 1898. But northern Uganda became very important when rumours spread that the French intended to capture it. The British feared that if France got hold of northern Uganda, the Nile would be diverted and this would interfere with their interests in Egypt.

In 1898 the British sent Macdonald to northern Uganda. He passed through Karamoja. He signed treaties of friendship and protection with the local chiefs whom he encountered in that region. Meanwhile, another expedition was led by Captain Austin. He travelled as far as Lake Rudolf. He signed many treaties which brought many chiefdoms under the British protectorate. A third expedition was led by Major Martyr who was instructed to get in touch with Kitchener at Fashoda. Martyr followed the Nile from Bunyoro and signed many treaties of protection. His expedition led to the formation of the Nile province in northern Uganda.

But it took much longer to establish the colonial administration in this part of Uganda. This was due to the following reasons:-

- The Protectorate government wanted to disarm the people, and to involve them in government without provoking their hostility.

- The government also had to divide the north into administrative units and to appoint agents to administer those units.

- They had to find and train local leaders so that indirect rule could be established.

Macdonald

- They had to convince the local people to begin growing new crops such as cotton and tobacco.

- They had to persuade the cattle keepers to think of land as having boundaries and therefore restrict their animals to certain areas only.

- They had to stop raiding, which was not easy.

Despite these hurdles, administrative stations were set up in order to ensure effective administration of the north. In Lango a station was built at Kumu and Palongo in 1909. In 1901 a station was built in Gulu, and in 1912 in Kitgum among the Acholi people. Another station was built in Arua among the Alur, Madi, Lugbara and Kakwa in 1914, and in 1918 on Moroto River. By 1920, only Karamoja was not under British colonial rule.

The central native councils were established in Acholi in 1914, Teso in 1916 and Lango in 1919. The northerners thereafter started to appreciate economic, medical and educational advantages of a peaceful, settled life.

It can be said that British control over the whole of Uganda was complete only after the drawing up of the current borders of the country. In 1902, the areas west of the Rift Valley were transferred to the British East Africa Protectorate. In 1914, the present-day West Nile district was transferred from Sudan to Uganda. The area around Kabale in Kigezi was transferred to Uganda from Congo in 1910. In 1914, the northern line constituting the border between Uganda and Sudan was also agreed upon.

Once the border of the protectorate was established in 1907, the responsibility for governing Uganda was transferred from the Foreign Office to the Colonial Office and the Commissioner became the Governor.

Revision 17

1 (a) Why did Semei Kakungulu collaborate with the British colonialists before 1914?

   (b) What were the results of this collaboration?

2 (a) What were the terms of the Buganda Agreement of 1900?

   (b) What effects did the agreement have on the people of Buganda?

3 (a) Why were the British interested in Uganda during the 19th century?

   (b) Giving examples, show how British rule was established in Uganda up to 1914.

4 (a) Why was Egypt interested in extending its rule into Uganda in the 19th century?

(b)   Describe the activities of either Samuel Baker or Charles Gordon in trying to establish Egyptian rule in Uganda.

(c)   What were the results of the Egyptian Sudanese activities up to 1875 on:-

(i)   Bunyoro, and

(ii) northern Uganda?

18

Reactions to the establishment of colonial rule in Uganda

The local people reacted to the establishment of colonial rule in two ways. One was collaboration and the other was outright resistance.

There were three important collaborators in Uganda, one of whom was Semei Kakungulu. Other prominent collaborators were Sir Apollo Kagwa and Nuwa Mbaguta.

Apollo Kagwa

Apollo Kagwa was one of the most outstanding collaborators with the British colonial authorities in Uganda. Born in 1869, Apollo Kagwa served as a page in the courts of Kabaka Mutesa and Mwanga. He therefore learnt the art of political survival in those dangerous times. He was converted to the Protestant faith and became one of the powerful Protestant leaders who played a big role in the downfall of Mwanga. In 1894, he supported Colonel Colville, a British Commissioner, against Kabalega of Bunyoro. In 1897, Kagwa, Stanislaus Mugwanya and Zakaria Kisingiri were appointed regents to rule on behalf of the infant Kabaka Daudi Chwa.

Sir Apollo Kagwa

Because he was seen as a good boy by the British colonialists, Kagwa was appointed Prime Minister (Katikkiro) of Buganda. In 1898, he led an armed force against mutinying Sudanese soldiers. He played a major role in the signing of the 1900 Buganda Agreement. He was one of the principal beneficiaries of that agreement because he was rewarded with 30 square miles of land for his work. Despite his early collaboration Kagwa did not hesitate to uphold the rights of the Lukiiko when they were breached by the British contrary to the provisions of the 1900 Buganda Agreement.

Apollo Kagwa also boosted education in Buganda by encouraging the establishment of schools. He further facilitated the development of agriculture by encouraging the adoption of new agricultural methods and new crops such as cotton. Between 1914 and 1916, he brought about a lot of reforms in the judicial, financial and administrative spheres in Buganda.

He also wrote a book, *Basekabaka Ba Buganda,* on the pre-colonial history of Buganda. However, owing to his occasional clashes with the British, he was forced to resign as Prime Minister of Buganda in 1926.

Nuwa Mbaguta

Like most great men in history, Nuwa Mbaguta was a man of very humble origins. Born in 1862 and a Munyankore by birth, he suffered greatly in his early life as an orphan. Nevertheless, his being an orphan did not in any way dampen his ambition. Mbaguta soon abandoned his relatives and went to seek his fortunes at the court of Ntare V. His rise to prominence did not take long. Because of his humble character and fearlessness, he was appointed guardian of the Omugabe's residence.

Full of courage and possessing a rich sense of humour, Mbaguta was praised by Omugabe's army even before he joined it. When he started his military career, he joined the Omugabe's favourite military unit. Immediately he became close to the Omugabe because of his skill in wrestling and his fearlessness. As a result, he was nicknamed Rutinwa, "the Feared One".

Nuwa Mbaguta

Mbaguta soon became very popular in the army. He participated in many military expeditions and he effectively mastered military and political skills. By the time the British reached Ankole, he was already a figure to reckon with. In 1894, he signed a treaty of friendship and protection with Major Cunningham, a British agent, on behalf of Ntare V. Upon the death of Ntare V in 1895, Mbaguta supported Kahaya's claim to the throne against Rwakatorogo. This was to work in his favour. In his shrewdness and far-sightedness, Mbaguta realised that the British had come to stay and therefore, unlike his friends who suspected their intentions in Nkore, he immediately co-operated with the British to ensure his own survival.

Mbaguta personally supervised the construction of the road which was to be used by the British Commissioner. In return for his services, he was appointed Prime Minister of Ankole, a position that had not existed before. From there on, Mbaguta assisted the British in furthering their colonial ambitions. He also brought all the chiefs under his control. With his assistance, the Ankole kingdom was expanded to include the kingdoms of Buhweju, Igara, part of Bunyaruguru, Kajara and parts of Mpororo. All those areas had become part of the Ankole kingdom by 1910.

Mbaguta worked tirelessly to bring both the southern and western parts of Uganda under British control. He boosted formal education by encouraging the establishment of mission schools in Ankole. By the time he retired from government in

1938, Mbaguta had done a lot of work for the welfare of his people. Mbaguta died in 1944, six years after his retirement from government service.

Kabalega of Bunyoro

Kabalega was the Omukama of Bunyoro. He ascended the throne in 1871 after defeating Kagumire, his rival. After succeeding his father, Kamurasi, he suppressed all his opponents and reorganised his army, the *abarusura*, into a professional force. The soldiers took orders only from the Omukama himself.

The abarusura was comprised of ten battalions consisting of one thousand to two thousand men each. They opened a new chapter in Bunyoro. They were distributed in all key positions to crush the old aristocrats and help in regaining the old boundaries of the ancient Bunyoro Empire. By the 1880s Kabalega had reasserted Bunyoro's authority in many parts of Uganda in a bid to revive the glory and extent of ancient Bunyoro-Kitara.

In the 1890s the expansionist policy of Kabalega brought him into conflict with the British imperialists who had come in full force to colonise East Africa. The armed conflict started in 1891. Kabalega's expansionism had deposed Kasagama of Toro from his throne. Kasagama had fled to Buganda where Lugard forced Kabalega's men out of Toro and restored Kasagama to his throne.

From 1892, Kabalega organised a skilful resistance to the British. He attacked the British forts which Lugard had built between Bunyoro and Toro, frequently interrupting their communication and cutting off their supplies. In 1893, the British withdrew from most of their forts in Toro. This withdrawal was recommended by Gerald Portal, a special British Commissioner. Kabalega got another chance to invade Toro and reoccupy it.

In late 1893, Colville invaded Bunyoro and set up many forts to secure the route to Lake Albert but Kabalega continuously attacked these forts. In 1894, Colville invaded Bunyoro again with a combined British – Buganda force of eight European officers, 400 Sudanese and 15,000 Baganda.

Because the Omukama made a serious strategic mistake by dividing his army into small units and spreading them thinly in his kingdom, Colville was able to advance without any difficulties.

Kabalega abandoned his Mparo capital and retreated to Budongo forest. He avoided serious engagements and his soldiers were only committed to rearguard action. He retreated across the Nile into Lango. Colville's invasion of Bunyoro in 1894 inflicted heavy losses on Kabalega's army. Bunyoro lost five and a half counties including Buyaga and Bugangaizi. All the lost counties were awarded to Buganda.

Economically, Bunyoro was ruined as farms and homes were destroyed by the invaders. Many of the abarusura officers surrendered and a few started collaborating with the British and were later appointed chiefs. However, the British occupation of Bunyoro was not the end of Kabalega. In 1895, he reorganised his army and launched attacks on the British troops. He returned from Lango and invaded Toro. He defeated the British-Buganda force at Kijumbura Island near Masindi and forced them to withdraw to Hoima.

In 1896, Bunyoro once again fell to British military might and was declared part of Uganda. Nevertheless, Kabalega continued his war of resistance in 1897. Although he was officially deposed in 1898 by the British, who set up a regency council to rule Bunyoro, Kabalega continued the war against to the British in the northern part of Bunyoro until it was conquered by a combined British-Indian force. Two of Kabalega's brilliant guerilla generals who led the resistance to the British invaders were Ireta and Kikulule.

Kabalega carried on the guerilla warfare until he was captured together with Mwanga at the border of Teso and Lango at a place called Kangai in 1899. The two kings were deported to Kismayu in northern Kenya and later transferred to the Seychelles in 1899 where Kabalega stayed until 1923. He was allowed to come back in 1923, but he was already about 73 years old. He died at Jinja, 50 miles east of Kampala.

Rwot Awich

Among the people who seriously resisted the imposition of colonial rule in Uganda was *Rwot* (Chief) Awich of the Payira chiefdom in Acholi. He succeeded his father, Rwot Camo, in the 1880s as Rwot.

Rwot Awich was a very courageous chief who usually raided the Paibona. It was his frequent raids of his neighbours which brought him into sharp conflict with the British. The British representative at Nimule, Major Radcliffe, tried to arrest Awich but all his efforts were frustrated by the chief's tactics. Radcliffe's attempts caused a rift between Awich and the British. Awich later granted political asylum to Kabalega and his soldiers. The British immediately assumed that Awich was assisting Kabalega by sending his own army to fight the British administration on Kabalega's behalf.

When the British demanded that Kabalega and his men be expelled from Payira, Awich refused to do so on the grounds that the chief of Payira was an independent sovereign who did not take orders from any power, including the British. This annoyed the British authorities who sent an expedition under Captain Harman against Awich. Rwot Awich was defeated in 1901 by a British-led force owing to their superior weapons. After Awich's defeat, he was arrested and imprisoned in Kampala.

After deposing Awich, the British failed to establish a strong government which could effectively replace his. The people of Payira gave the British a lot of headache by persistently demanding the reinstatement of their ruler. In 1902, Rwot Awich was brought back to Payira from Kampala and reinstated. The following year, he refused to sign an agreement with the British representative, Major Macdonald.

Despite the fact that all other rulers around Payira had already surrendered to the British, Awich did not. He continued to resist British rule. Awich once more helped in the inter-clan wars on the side of the Jo clan of Puranga against the Langi Ogoo clan. Because of this action, Rwot Awich was fined ivory, cattle and goats by the District Commissioner.

Later there was an allegation that Awich was stockpiling guns from the Arab traders and he was tried at Nimule. Awich who had a very hot temper, boxed one of the court prosecutors, a European, during the court proceedings. Awich was fined two cows and imprisoned in Kampala for contempt of court. During his absence, his chiefdom was divided into two. By the time Awich came back in 1919, his chiefdom was no more. Despite his resistance against the British colonialists, Awich invited the missionaries to spread Christianity and educate his people.

Revision 18

1   Describe the careers and achievements of:-

   (i)   Apollo Kagwa

   (ii)   Nuwa Mbaguta

   (iii)   Chief Awich

2   (a)   Describe the methods used by the British to establish their rule over Uganda.

   (b)   How did the people of Uganda react to British rule?

3   Describe the response of the following to colonial occupation of their areas:-

   (a)   Chief Awich

   (b)   Kabaka Mwanga

   (c)   Kasagama of Toro

4   (a)   Why were the British interested in Uganda in the 19th century?

   (b)   Giving examples, show how British rule was established in Uganda up to 1914.

5   Show how Omukama Kabalega responded to the threat of European occupation of his kingdom.

19

British conquest of Kenya

The land at the coast of East Africa had for long been under the Sultan of Zanzibar. He owned almost all the coastal towns. At the time of the partition, there were only two powers who wanted East Africa: the British and the Germans. There had already been an attempt by King Leopold II of Belgium to colonise East Africa on the pretext of stopping slave trade in Congo.

King Leopold II sent an expedition to establish a route from the East Coast into the interior, but after receiving Stanley's reports, he decided to penetrate Congo from the Atlantic Ocean. This created a sense of panic among Europeans who were interested in the coast of East Africa.

As we have already noted, Johnston, with the permission of the Sultan of Zanzibar, signed treaties with chiefs in the Kilimanjaro area on behalf of the British commercial groups. The newly created Association of British East Africa headed by William Mackinnon was ready to take over and exploit the area acquired by Johnston, but this was not yet possible because their plan was not supported by Britain.

In 1884, Carl Peters arrived in the area and concluded many treaties with the chiefs of Usagara, Uzigua, Nguru and Ukami. When Carl Peters went back to Germany, Bismarck declared that area part of the German sphere of influence. To prevent the prospect of Anglo-German conflict in East Africa, the British and Germans signed the Anglo-German Agreement of 1886. Under the terms of this agreement, Zanzibar, Pemba, Mafia, Lamu and the towns of Kismayu, Brava and Merca became dominions of the Sultan of Zanzibar.

As we have already seen during the partition of East Africa, the agreement of 1886 divided the land between River Ruvuma and the Tana by a line from the Umba River to the south-eastern shore of Lake Victoria. The area south of the line became the German sphere of influence and the northern part came under British influence. Under the terms of the 1890 agreement, Uganda became part of the British dominion in East Africa whose centre was moved from Mombasa to Nairobi.

The traders, missionaries and administrators were not interested in the interior of Kenya. They only had an interest in Uganda. Therefore, from 1907 up to around 1917, they tended to neglect the hinterland of Kenya and concentrated on Uganda. However, the Imperial British East Africa Company had established their customs stations at Kismayu, Malindi, Vanga, Lamu, Vitu and Takaungu. They also established sub-stations in the interior at Machakos, Fort Smith (Dagoretti) and Mumias. The Protectorate Government also established Meru, Chuka, Nandi, Archer's Post, Mount Kulal, Ngabotok, Serenetic and Wajir. It is worth noting that by 1914, most of Kenya was still not under effective British rule.

Reactions to the establishment of colonial rule in Kenya

There were two different types of African reaction to the establishment of British rule in Kenya. Some people collaborated with the British while others resisted them outright. Collaborators were people such as Nabongo Mumia and Lenana, and the resisters included Sandeyo.

Nabongo Mumia

Nabongo means 'ruler'. So Nabongo Mumia meant 'Chief Mumia'. Born probably in 1849 at Lureko, Nabongo Mumia was a ruler of the Luhya (Wanga) kingdom. He was a renowned, peaceful leader who was highly praised by the British imperialists when they came across him in the late 19th century. He was deeply interested in trade with the coastal traders. During the era of colonialism, Nabongo Mumia recognised the power of the British guns. He therefore welcomed the British imperialists and allowed them to operate from his capital.

From Mumia's capital, a series of expeditions were sent out against other people between 1894 and 1906. Nabongo himself provided the British with soldiers and guides. For instance, expeditions were sent out against the Luo, the Nandi and the Bukusu. His army fought alongside the British force which was composed of Baganda, Sudanese and British officers to extend British administration in Kenya. As a sign of appreciation for his co-operation, the British extended his sphere of influence by making him a paramount chief in the Wanga kingdom. Mumia's followers were also recruited as agents to administer other parts of Kenya. Nabongo died at an advanced age in 1949.

The British and the Maasai
When Laibon Mbatian of the Purko Maasai died in 1890, he left his two sons, Lenana and Sendeyo, as rivals for his throne. Sendeyo went away towards the Loita region of northern Tanzania. Lenana stayed in the area between Ngong and Naivasha.

Sendeyo became a thorn in the flesh of Lenana. He constantly sent his army to raid Lenana's territory. To make matters worse, famine and diseases seriously affected both Lenana's people and their cattle. Rinderpest destroyed Lenana's animals and he had to look for asylum for some Maasai women and children in Kikuyuland. Unfortunately, when he went back to reclaim them, he found that many of them had been sold to slave traders.

All these problems made Lenana very desperate and, in 1894, he sought help from the British.

The British and Lenana
Lenana was one of the Kenyan collaborators with the British. He requested assistance from the British at Fort Smith in 1894. The British in this fort were under the command of the British agent, Francis Hall. Francis Hall was very pleased with him. Lenana allowed the British to build their railway line across his territory without causing them any problems. His men helped the British in raids against those who did not

co-operate. As a result of his collaboration with the British, Lenana's fame increased. The British rewarded him with cattle and he successfully consolidated his power. The cordial relations between the Maasai and the British were soured. However, Sir Charles Eliot, the British Commissioner from 1900-1904, despised the Maasai way of life. Furthermore he considered them toothless and therefore not a threat to the British anymore.

The Maasai Agreement was signed in 1904, in which the Maasai were to be moved to two reserved areas of Ngong in the south and the Laikipia plateau in the north. They were promised that the two areas were theirs as long as the Maasai race existed. However, this promise was not kept by the British. The white settlers demanded more land and this resulted in the 1911 agreement. Under this agreement, all Maasai from Laikipia were moved to Ngong. The British were prepared to use force to quell any Maasai resistance.

The British and the Nandi

By the 19th century the Nandi had become very powerful at the expense of the neighbouring Maasai. They were opposed to British rule. They did not even allow British travellers to pass through their country. A British trader who attempted to travel through Nandiland was brutally murdered in 1895. His name was West. When the British sent their force to avenge the death of West, they were defeated and those who survived the Nandi spears fled in disarray.

For eleven years, the Nandi put up a stiff resistance against the British. They knew their forested hill country well and so they could strike the enemy and melt back into the forests. For long, they defied the British, looting the railway depots and even the railway lines, and removing the telephone wires.

The Nandi were only subdued in 1905 when a British commander, Colonel Meinertzhagen, visited Koitasel arap Samoe, the Nandi leader (*Orkoiyot*). When Samoei came out to greet his visitors, he was shot dead together with his aides. When the British government set up a commission of enquiry, Meinertzhagen pleaded that he shot Samoei in self-defence but, to the Nandi, this was deliberate murder. The death of the leaders disheartened the community and this enabled the British to sweep through Nandiland and crush all resistance. The Nandi were moved to a reserve far away from the railway and their land was allocated to the British settlers.

Revision 19

1 (a) Why did Nandi resistance against the British fail?

  (b) What were the consequences of their resistance?

2 What was the relationship between the British and the
  (a) Maasai, (b) Nandi during the late 19th century?

3 (a) Describe the methods used by the British to extend their rule in Kenya.

  (b) How did the Kenyan peoples react to their rule?

4 Describe the careers of the following people:-

  (a) Nabongo Mumia

  (b) Lenana

5 (a) Describe the response of the Nandi to the stablishment of colonial rule in their area.

  (b) Why were African societies unable to stop White colonial rule in Africa?

20

German East Africa (Tanganyika)

The man whose efforts led to the acquisition of present-day Tanzania by the Germans was Carl Peters. He was a German colonialist who arrived in Zanzibar in 1884 with some two German friends. They crossed to the mainland disguised as mechanics and signed treaties with the chiefs of Uzigua, Nguru and Ukami. When the Berlin Conference of 1884-85 stipulated effective occupation, the three Germans formed an association called the Society for German Colonisation. They secured treaties including those obtained through blood-brotherhood. These treaties were approved by Bismarck in 1885.

Immediately afterwards, this society was christened German East Africa Company, and it was given a charter to rule over German East Africa with Carl Peters as its head.

German ships forced the Sultan of Zanzibar to accept that all goods leaving the coast of East Africa had to pass through the points controlled by the Germans.

There was already very intense rivalry between the IBEA Co. and the German East Africa Co. by this time. This forced the two powers, i.e. the British and Germans, to sign an agreement in 1886. This agreement was the Anglo-German Agreement.

Under the terms of this agreement, the area extending from south of River Umba up to Mt Kilimanjaro and to the eastern shores of Lake Victoria became the German sphere of influence and the northern part became the British sphere of influence.

When rivalry over Uganda became intense between the Germans and the British, another agreement was signed in 1890, through which the British took over Uganda and in return Germany got Heligoland. The border between Uganda and Tanganyika was also fixed.

On 18th November 1890, British dominion was declared over Zanzibar, and Germany now had direct control over Tanganyika.

Tanganyika under German East Africa Company's administration

Carl Peters, the head of the company, received a charter from the German emperor in 1885. A committee was appointed to help in managing German affairs in East Africa. Between 1884 and 1886, the company sent out many expeditions in order to extend their supremacy in the interior of East Africa. Later on, the company raised its flag at the coastal towns, and the Germans had established their base at Dar es Salaam by 1887. As they continued to extend their influence along the coast, they sparked off two dangerous revolts owing to their interference with the coastal trade and *hongo*, the duties imposed on caravans in transit.

Abushiri revolt (1888 - 1890)

Several reasons were responsible for the Abushiri revolt.

- When the Germans signed an agreement with the Sultan of Zanzibar on 28th April 1888, the Liwali of Dar es Salaam was sent to all coastal towns with the German flag to impose German administration. The coastal people were forced to resist German occupation.

- The coastal peoples also feared that the Germans were going to interfere with their commercial interests, mainly the slave trade and hongo, the ivory and the rubber trade.

- The war started immediately after Abushiri ibn Salim al-Hathi, a member of an Arab family, had held a meeting at a plantation outside Pangani. The family feared that the Germans would take their land. The meeting decided that war be declared on the Germans.

Abushiri, born to an Arab father and a Galla mother, belonged to the Hanth clan. In 1888, he was 40 years old. He was wanted in Zanzibar in connection with the heavy debts he had failed to pay. He had furthermore shown disrespect to the Sultan by selling some land in Zanzibar to the Germans.

The Abushiri revolt comprised three separate attempts to drive out the Germans: one led by Abushiri on the northern coast, i.e. around Port Pangani, another at the southern ports of Dar-es-Salaam, Kilwa and Lindi, and the third in Uzigua under Bwana Heri.

The Abushiri revolt which started in September 1888, was entirely spontaneous. Since the Germans were unprepared, they were defeated and driven out of all the coastal towns except Bagamayo and Dar-es-Salaam. A few company officials were killed. Abushiri's followers came from among the armed slaves, caravan traders and from the Diwani who had lost power during the 19th century.

Abushiri was joined in the revolt by an African leader of Swahili origin, Bwana Heri, chief of Zigua. However, this revolt failed because the Germans received reinforcements from their government. The reinforcements included Sudanese soldiers, Zulu from Port Mozambique, Somalis, Turkish police and a large number of Tanganyika *askaris*. All these were under the leadership of Wissman Herman.

Wissman conquered the northern coastal towns first. Abushiri retreated to the interior, where he hired five thousand Maviti. Unfortunately, they were not helpful at all. They looted property belonging to the local people and deserted Abushiri. Consequently, Abushiri lost support in the interior as a result of Maviti activities.

In 1889 Abushiri, who had already been deserted by most of his followers, was betrayed to the Germans by a village headman in Usagara. He was captured by the Germans and hanged in Bagamoyo.

In 1890, Wissman captured the southern towns and turned north to deal with Bwana Heri. But Bwana Heri continued to resist the Germans until he surrendered as a result of the famine of 1888-92 that stuck north-eastern Tanzania.

Reasons for the failure of the Abushiri revolt

- The Germans had very superior weapons. Their guns included the Maxim gun, whereas the Africans and the Arabs possessed only daggers and spears.

- The Abushiri rebellion was very unco-ordinated. Abushiri himself had no contact with Mataro or Bwana Heri.

- The German army was highly disciplined compared to that of Abushiri which was unruly and ill-trained.

- Abushiri himself was not a very good general. He employed wrong strategies in the face of superior German weapons, e.g. he fought pitched battles with the Germans instead of engaging in guerilla warfare.

- The Germans had African allies such as Kigo Mkubwa, a Zigua chief who supplied the Germans with troops and guides.

- The Maviti also led to the crushing of the Abushiri rebellion. They made Abushiri lose support in the interior by looting property belonging to the local people.

- The weakness within Abushiri's army led to the failure of the revolt. Abushiri's soldiers deserted Abushiri, hence leading to his capture and hanging by the Germans.

- When Abushiri was killed, Bwana Heri had been weakened by famine which killed many of his soldiers. He had to surrender in 1890.

Results of the revolt

- The withdrawal of the charter from the German East Africa Company by the German government. The German government accused the company of being too harsh on the people under their jurisdiction.

- The German government took over the running of Tanganyika from the company.

- The German East Africa Company failed to extend German influence to the interior owing to lack of capital to finance it.

- Depopulation, as many people were killed in the wars.

- The Germans realised that the Africans were a force to reckon with. If German administration was to succeed, the Africans had to be included in the system.

- Devastation of towns and houses, leaving many people without shelter and food.

- Human suffering as many people ran for their lives, and hence disruption of family ties.

Establishment of German colonial rule in Tanganyika

The German government took over Tanganyika because the German East Africa Company had failed to control that territory. Tanganyika was declared a German territory in 1890 under the Foreign Ministry. The German government appointed a Commissioner to govern the territory.

In due course, the territory was transferred from the Foreign Ministry to the Council Office and the Commissioner became Governor. The German government therefore took over the direct administration of Tanganyika on 1 January 1891 after crushing the Abushiri revolt.

Right from the start, German occupation of Tanganyika was largely through use of military force. Other methods which were rarely used were agreements, land settlement and collection of taxes.

German rule and Hehe resistance

In the late 1880s the leader of the Hehe of Tanzania was Mkwawa. He was preoccupied with extending his administration to the neighbouring areas. But his imperial expansion coincided with the imperial expansion of the Germans into the interior of East Africa.

Mkwawa was slender, quick, intelligent, unpredictable, suspicious and cruel. He was too proud to submit to the Germans without resistance. Therefore, from the outset, war between the Germans and the Hehe became inevitable.

Although Mkwawa tried to negotiate with the Germans, his envoys were mistaken for warriors and killed.

In retaliation, Mkwawa organised an ambush. His men, using spears at close range, rendered the gunpower of the Germans ineffective and killed 310 German troops, including all their porters and Zelewski, the German commander. Only 60 of Mkwawa's men died on the spot and 200 died of wounds later. After this military encounter, Mkwawa closed the trade route which ran through his country.

When the Germans attacked Mkwawa's city in 1894 and captured it he escaped, and in the next four years, he engaged the Germans in guerilla warfare. He was, however, tracked down in 1898 but rather than surrender to the Germans he shot himself.

Reasons for Mkwawa's defeat

- The Germans were well supplied with guns compared to Mkwawa who had only a few.

- The German forces were well fed compared to the ill-fed army of Mkwawa.

- Rifts among Mkwawa's chiefs also led to his defeat. Much as he wanted to fight the Germans to the last man, some of his chiefs were not prepared to do so.

- Some of Mkwawa's neighbours sided with the Germans.

- There was lack of unity in his empire.

- Mkwawa's army was not a disciplined one. They were very harsh on their own people.

After the defeat of Mkwawa, the Germans built forts at all strategic points and started demanding taxes from the Hehe people. This ushered in a new period of administration.

German occupation of Makonde

The occupation of the Makonde plateau was also by force of arms. The indigenous people of Makonde were the Yao. The chief of the Yao people was called Machembo. He defeated many German expeditions until he was overcome in 1899.

German occupation of Unyanyembe

The area around Tabora was occupied by the Nyamwezi of Unyanyembe. Its chief was Isike. Like Mkwawa and Machembo, Isike put up a stiff resistance to the Germans. Though he defeated many German expeditions, he was overpowered in January 1893. He committed suicide rather than fall into the hands of the Germans and be tortured.

Resistance also broke out in some other areas of Tanganyika, for instance among the Gogo and the Chagga of Moshi. Similarly, after the Belgians had withdrawn from Rwanda and Burundi, Mwesi Kisabo, the ruler of Burundi, resisted the establishment of German rule until he surrendered in 1903. However, not all African chiefs and their subjects resisted the imposition of German colonialism. For example, most Bahaya chiefs in Bukoba accepted German rule peacefully.

Revision 20

1   How did the Germans administer Tanganyika up to 1914?

2   Describe the general response of the Tanganyika people to the imposition of colonial rule in their areas.

3   (a)   What problems did Abushiri face during his resistance to German rule?

    (b)   How did his resistence affect the peoples of Tanganyika?

21

Zanzibar and the British (1900-1914)

By 1900, Zanzibar had already been in contact with the British and other European powers for a long time. As a result, when the British declared Zanzibar their protectorate in 1890, the Sultan Ali bin Said may not have understood what the treaty of protection meant. What followed was that the Sultan was allowed to continue holding his post but the responsibility for external matters was passed on to the British.

Initially, Zanzibar was placed under the authority of the Commissioner and British Consul General whose headquarters was at Mombasa. But as the Mombasa-based Consul General was very busy with the affairs of the mainland, Zanzibar became the responsibility of the Consul General on the island, who was also the First Minister to the Sultan.

The British Consul General in Zanzibar was appointed as a regent in 1902, when seventeen-year-old Sultan Seyyid Ali ascended the throne. Consul General Rogers used his position and influence to initiate a lot of changes, including the appointment of a finance adviser to the Sultan.

In 1905 Edward Clarke, a financial adviser, came to Zanzibar and proposed the reorganisation of the administration in the areas of finance, judiciary, communications and education. The Departments of Education and Agriculture were set up, the latter with the aim of improving the yield and quality of Zanzibar's two main crops, cloves and coconuts. In 1911, Kiswahili replaced Arabic in government schools. Arab families were no longer regarded as important in government. They resented many of the changes but there was nothing they could do about it.

Europeans poured into Zanzibar in order to implement Rogers' proposals. Ali ibn Hamed, who was educated in

167

European ways, found himself powerless and he abdicated. He was replaced by Khalifa. In 1913 control of Zanzibar was moved to the Colonial Office. The British agent in Zanzibar became a Resident with complete control over the administration of the island.

The Resident was supposed to report to the Governor of British East Africa, something which elicited a lot of complaints from Sayid Khalifa. Khalifa feared that the British wanted to merge Zanzibar with the Kenyan mainland. As a result of his bitter complaints, the British set up a Protectorate Council with the Sultan as its president. But even then, real authority in Zanzibar remained in the hands of British colonial officials.

Political, economic and constitutional developments in Zanzibar after First World War

Unlike its immediate neighbour Tanganyika, Zanzibar was not seriously affected by the First World War. In the 1920s Zanzibar was like any other British colony in the world. In 1926 Executive and Legislative Councils were established. The Legislative Council comprised three Arabs, two Indians, and one European, who were the official members. There were also ten Europeans who were the unofficial members of the Legislative Council.

No African member was nominated to the Legislative Council until 1945. This was mainly because the British looked at Zanzibar purely as an Arab settlement, so only Arabs were encouraged to participate in government. This discrimination against Africans caused a lot of problems and hostility in the latter history of Zanzibar. The Arabs formed the landowning aristocracy headed by Sultan Khalifa II who ruled Zanzibar from 1911 to 1960.

In 1927, the Arabs formed the Clove Growers Association in order to defend their political and economic interests. This body became powerful enough to win support from the British government when the clove growers were hit by a world-wide economic depression between 1929 and 1935. The government

168

imposed a new export tax at the expense of the Indian and European traders who handled much of the export trade in Zanzibar to help the Clove Growers Association.

In 1937, the Indians threatened to withdraw completely from clove trade. This would have led to the economic collapse of the clove-based economy. Fortunately for Zanzibar, the British Resident intervened and worked out a compromise acceptable both to the clove growers and the Indian traders.

22

The building of Uganda Railway

The railway from Mombasa to Kisumu (and eventually to Kampala) was called the Uganda Railway because it was primarily constructed to link Uganda with the East African coast. At the time, Uganda was the focus of British interests in East Africa. The intervening country, later called Kenya, did not then appear to offer much opportunity for trade. The line was surveyed by J.R.L. Macdonald in 1892. The costs of constructing the railway were grossly underestimated. Originally, it was estimated that the railway would cost £2 million. In the end, it cost £8 million.

Reasons for construction of Uganda Railway

- The railway was needed to facilitate British administration in Uganda, especially after the declaration of the Uganda Protectorate in 1894.

- There was a strategic reason also. The British wanted to control Uganda, which is the source of the Nile. The Nile was the lifeline of Egypt, which in turn was the key to the Suez Canal sea route to British India.

- The construction of the Uganda Railway was also needed not only to establish effective administration in Kenya and Uganda but also to promote the economic development of the two countries.

- Uganda's soil was found to be very fertile and particularly good for cotton and coffee, which the British wanted to grow there for use in their home industries.

- The British also wanted a market for their surplus manufactured goods.

- The British wanted to abolish the slave trade in the interior of East Africa.

The labour for construction came from India: the Indian coolies. Many of the skilled craftsmen and the clerical staff were also brought from India. Africans, who were quite contented with their way of life, were not willing to do construction work and, in some instances, they were downright hostile to the railway project.

Some parliamentarians in Britain opposed the idea of constructing the Uganda Railway because they doubted whether it was economically viable. Some of them even dismissed the planned railway as 'the lunatic line'.

The construction of Uganda Railway

The first rail was laid on the mainland opposite Mombasa in 1896 under the supervision of George Whitehouse, a British engineer. Thirty-five Indian coolies built embankments and bridges, made cuttings and culverts as the railway crawled up through the coastal hills and straightened out for the semi-desert of Taru. On 30 May 1897 the railway line reached Voi near the Taita Hills.

Beyond Voi it started to ascend again, reaching Tsavo where the railway workers encountered the man-eating lions. This was in 1898. At Tsavo, the lions caused panic, entering the camps at night and seizing their victims while they slept. However, the lions were eventually hunted down and shot by Colonel Patterson.

After two years, the line reached the edge of the Rift Valley where a base camp was built. This camp constituted the beginning of the Kenyan capital city, Nairobi, which means 'cold' in Maasai. The railway reached Nairobi in June 1899.

The Rift Valley escarpment presented the engineers with a challenge. They overcame this by constructing a vertical incline down which supplies and locomotives could be lowered on a specially made platform. The Rift Valley was at last crossed in 1900, but that same year, the constructors had problems with Nandi raiders, who cut off the telegraph wires.

The Nandi resented the growing British interference with their traditional way of life. They stole rails, bolts, sleepers, and wires which were valuable sources of iron which they highly treasured. Although the Nandi raids slowed down the pace of construction, the railhead eventually reached Kisumu in 1901. A steamer ship now plied Lake Victoria between Buganda and Kisumu.

Problems met by constructors

- Formidable physical obstacles such as the waterless Nyika plains, where drinking water was very scarce.

- Some hills on the East African plateau had to be dug through.

- Some steep escarpments, mainly the numerous river beds, were difficult to bridge.

- They had to construct some inclines which could be used to lower the supplies and locomotives.

- At Tsavo, lions ate some of the workers.

- Much human misery was also caused by malaria, small pox and jiggers. The coolies did not know how to deal with jiggers so the jiggers were allowed to grow mature in their feet and even their buttocks, causing them a lot of pain.

- Food and drinking water were always in short supply.

- Hostile tribes such as the Nandi frequently cut off wires and even the rails to make ornaments.

- Lack of reliable communications as a result of the disruption of telegraph lines made it difficult to provide medical care in time in order to prevent the spread of diseases like small pox, which caused numerous deaths.

Effects of Uganda Railway

- The high cost of the construction of the Uganda Railway forced the British to seriously embark on the development of the area to justify this expenditure.

- The railway helped to generate new commercial possibilities. European and Indian traders were attracted inland, and towns developed. The development of important towns such as Nairobi, Nakuru and Kisumu are attributed to the construction of the Uganda Railway.

- The railway linked Uganda and Kenya to the outside world.

- It also facilitated the consolidation of British administration of Uganda. The movement of soldiers and administrators became very easy.

- For the first time, the possibility of the development of cash crops such as cotton and coffee was achieved. The new crops could be introduced and monitored easily.

- The Uganda Railway also led to the economic exploitation of Uganda as cotton and coffee were easily transported to the coast, then to Europe.

- The influx of the Europeans into East Africa brought with it Western civilisation, e.g. schools were built, and western culture was adopted by the Africans.

- The railway also promoted the money economy through trade. The development of towns brought some social problems such as prostitution which previously did not exist in Uganda, and East Africa in general.

- It also promoted the building of feeder roads. All these roads were meant to link up with the railway.

- It provided an easy means of transport from one point to another.

- African lives changed significantly as people abandoned their villages and began to trade and live in towns.

23

British indirect rule in Uganda

When the British occupied Uganda, they adopted the system of indirect rule in Uganda for two reasons. First, the British government did not have adequate human and financial resources to administer the protectorate directly. Secondly, the British feared that direct rule might lead to confrontation with the African people.

Origin of indirect rule

The concept of indirect rule was first developed by Lord Lugard in his book, *The Dual Mandate in Tropical Africa*. Indirect rule was applied in India, Uganda and Northern Nigeria. By definition, indirect rule means foreign rule through the indigenous rulers.

The idea behind indirect rule was to govern Africans through their traditional institutions. It was also believed that both the Africans and the British would benefit from this policy. It aimed at maintaining African chiefs as much as possible and, at the same time, educating them and developing their local administration into efficient organs of British colonialism.

Reasons for indirect rule

- It was cheap. The British government lacked funds to implement direct rule. For instance, they were given only 500 pounds annually to spend in India, Uganda and Nigeria. Indirect rule was not one of several alternatives from which the British had to choose but a necessity which could not be dodged if they were to rule over the Africans effectively.

- Indirect rule was considered the best means by which Africans could be trained and given the opportunity to manage their own affairs.

- The British could not recruit enough British personnel to administer all their colonies. For instance, in 1900 Lugard had only 42 officers and a very small army at his command in Northern Nigeria and Uganda.

- The British also realised that taking over power from traditional rulers would culminate in resistance. So the only fairly safe option was to rule through local agents.

- Indirect rule was also chosen because the British knew that they would not be blamed by the local people in case of colonial order. The local leaders would be seen as the ones responsible and they would take the blame without any resentment against the British.

- Africans could understand their fellow Africans better since they spoke the same languages. This would be a relief to the British administrators who would find it difficult to learn African languages within such a short time in order to better administer their colonies.

- The communication network, especially the transport system was very poor, so it was easier to rule the vast land through local agents.

Administrative structure of indirect rule

The Kiganda model of administration was adopted and used in various parts of the protectorate. Baganda agents were also used in some parts of the country. The hierarchy of administration was, from top to bottom:

a) Governor

b) Provincial Commissioner

c) District Commissioner

d) Assistant District Commissioner

e) Saza chiefs (county chiefs)

f) Gombolola chiefs (sub-county chiefs)

g) Muluka chiefs (parish chiefs)

h) Mutongole chiefs (sub-parish chiefs)

i) Village chiefs

The local rulers usually took orders from the British representatives in the districts. The main functions of these rulers were:

1. maintain law and order.

2. regulate and control the consumption of alcohol.

3. assist in the collection of taxes.

4. recruit labour for public works.

5. assist in the enforcement of government measures including anything from disease control to improving agriculture.

6. take part in the activities of the local courts, within defined limits and subject to the Commissioner's powers of review and correction.

It is worth noting that the British officials always intervened when the chiefs abused their powers.

Results of indirect rule
- It enabled the colonial officials to administer a very large area though they were thin on the ground.

- It promoted native authorities and native courts which became the model in Uganda and other colonies in Africa.

- The policy preserved the traditional systems at the expense of the development of modern state institutions.

- It promoted disunity as different ethnic groups were left to develop individually.

- It caused corruption and oppression of the natives as the chiefs misused their powers by collecting taxes for their own personal ends.

- Indirect rule was dictatorial as the chiefs were appointed by and answerable to the British.

- The use of local rulers to govern the natives eliminated the possibilities of popular rebellions against British colonialism.

Problems met by British administrators before 1914

- The British lacked qualified manpower. So it was not easy for them to administer their colonies effectively except where indirect rule was applied.

- Their work was hampered by inadequate means of communication.

- The British did not understand most of the indigenous languages and they were frequently misinterpreted, making their work very difficult.

- The local leaders were illiterate. This affected the flow of information.

- There also existed different systems of administration in the various parts of Uganda at the time the British came. Therefore it was a problem for the British to persuade other areas to accept the Kiganda system of administration.

- People were divided into *Wa-Ingereza*, *Wa-Faransa*, Muslims and traditionalists and relations between them were not always cordial. Therefore, it was not very easy for them to rule without getting involved in wars.

- There was resistance against imperialism, for example the rebellion in Acholi (Lamogi rebellion) and that of Kabalega.

- Some of the agents of the British were very unpopular. For instance, the Baganda were very unpopular in Bunyoro, and so were Semei Kakungulu and his agents in eastern Uganda, especially in present-day Tororo district.

- The funds at the disposal of the British administrators were meagre. This made their work very difficult, and it partly promoted corruption among their agents who had to grab things from the natives in order to pay themselves.

- It was not easy to convince people to grow cash crops which could generate income to run the protectorate.

- Tropical diseases afflicted some of the British administrators. For example, they succumbed to sleeping sickness in Buganda and Busoga.

Revision 21, 22 & 23

1   Describe the political, economic and constitutional development of Zanzibar up to 1940.

2   (a)   What were the difficulties faced by the builders of the Uganda Railway?

    (b)   How were the people of Uganda affected by its construction?

3   To which part of Uganda and for what reasons was the railway extended between 1920 and 1962?

4   What were the problems met during the construction of the Kenya-Uganda railway?

5   (a)   Why was the Uganda Railway built?

    (b)   Describe the development of the railway system in Uganda between 1912 and 1945.

6   (a)   Describe the development of the railway system in Kenya and Uganda up to 1945.

    (b)   Show its importance in the development of these countries during the same period.

8 (a) What was indirect rule?

   (b) Why did the British apply it in Uganda?

9 (a) Describe the British system of administration in Uganda before 1914.

   (b) What problems did the British face in their administration?

24

German administration in Tanganyika up to 1914

When the Germans took complete control of Tanganyika from the German East African Company in 1891, they adopted the system of direct rule. At the top of the administration was the Governor, who had far-reaching powers and authority over the territory. The Governor was directly answerable to the German Colonial Minister.

Just below the Governor in the administrative hierarchy was the Governor's Council which was introduced in 1904. The Council was responsible for advising the Governor on how to run the territory.

Below the Council were the district officers whose responsibilities included:

1. Overseeing the implementation of government policies.

2. Collecting taxes.

3. Appointing and dismissing African chiefs.

4. Presiding over courts and administering punishment accordingly.

5. Commanding the police force to maintain law and order.

In order to facilitate administration, Tanganyika had been divided into about twenty-two districts by 1914. At the bottom of the administrative ladder were the *jumbes* and *akidas* who reported to the District Commissioner. The jumbes and akidas were the literate Arabs who were imposed as chiefs in villages.

During the early decades of German colonial rule, road construction was of paramount importance to the administrators. Accordingly, they always forced the Africans to work on the roads without payment. In the process of obtaining this free labour, the jumbes and akidas were very callous and brutal. The Germans as well as the akidas and jumbes despised Africans and showed them little respect.

The Germans intended to make a lot of profit from the territory within the shortest time possible, so they introduced plantation agriculture and forced the Africans to work on the plantations. Cotton was grown in Mahenge and Iringa districts. The Germans put the two districts under military administration and this sparked off the outbreak of the Maji Maji rebellion.

The German administrators were brutal, cruel and harsh in their methods of administration. They were very arrogant and considered themselves a superior race that could not condescend to mix with the Africans. It was this attitude that partly triggered off the Maji Maji rebellion.

The Maji Maji uprising (1905 - 1907)

Background
Administering Tanganyika had made the Germans incur a lot of costs. In a bid to alleviate the heavy costs of running their territory, the Germans initiated development projects such as cotton growing. The projects, according to them, would help to generate funds to help in the running of the administration as well as producing raw cotton for the German textile industry.

The Germans used three methods to achieve these objectives. One of these was to introduce experimental projects along River Pangani and in the areas around Usambara, Kilimanjaro and Meru; a railway line to serve these projects was built from Tanga in 1891, and it reached Mombo in 1905 and Moshi in 1911. Secondly, they employed African labourers to assist the Germans in farming. Thirdly, they forced Africans to grow cash crops so that they could pay taxes.

Resentment against the Germans steadily built up until it erupted in 1905 among the Pogoro people of Kitope who refused to pick cotton and rioted, taking the Germans by surprise.

Causes of Maji Maji

'Maji' means water in Swahili. The name 'Maji Maji' was used to refer to the uprising in southern Tanganyika led by Kinjikitile. He claimed that his followers would be immune to German bullets if their bodies were sprinkled with water. Several factors were responsible for the outbreak of the Maji Maji rebellion.

- The Africans deeply hated growing cotton because it interfered with their normal routine and, besides, it was not doing well.

- The meagre profits which were realised by the Africans had to be shared with the headman who received 1/3 of the profits. This greatly angered the Africans.

- The production of cotton was brutally monitored.

- Africans were forced to work on the cotton farms of the Germans without payment. This angered the Africans and they therefore yearned to be free from such treatment.

- The jumbes and akidas were harsh to Africans, whom they even flogged in public. This was a humiliating and an intolerable act.

- The Africans had to pay a tax of three rupees, yet getting the rupees was not easy. They therefore felt that they were already caught up in some sort of slavery, hence they wished to become free.

- The akida and jumbe tax collectors were foreigners who were deeply resented by the Africans.

- The replacement of the African rulers with the akidas and jumbes.

- The arrogance of the Germans towards the Africans. For instance, the Germans considered themselves superior to Africans whom they viewed as unintelligent savages that did not deserve humane treatment, let alone equality.

- Disrespect for African culture by the Germans. For instance, flogging an African chief in public was something the Africans found outrageous.

- The Africans also had grievances against the akidas who were having affairs with their wives.

- The Germans had no respect for the religious beliefs of the Africans. For instance, the Germans would walk into the mosques with their dogs, an act which is condemned by the Koran.

- Africans wanted to regain their independence. That is why, when the rioting started, all the African tribes in southern Tanganyika united to fight the common enemy, the Germans, and their agents the jumbes and akidas.

- Kinjikitile's prophecies that his water would make them bulletproof encouraged Africans to rebel against German rule.

The course of the uprising

It began in July 1905 when the Porogo people of Kitope refused to pick cotton. This was followed by spontaneous revolts in many parts of southern Tanganyika. From the Rufiji area, the uprising spread to Uhunguru, Mehenga, and the Lukuledi and Kilombero valleys. The rebellion thus united the Ngindo, Mbuga, Pogoro and Ngoni.

On 31st July 1905 the Matumbi drove the hated akidas and all foreigners away from their hills. Plantations, missions, administrative *bomas* and Swahili shops were attacked and destroyed. All this took the Germans unawares.

The Maji Maji uprising was unique because it brought together many tribes in a common rebellion. What bound all these people together was their belief in the power of traditional religion. A medicineman, Kinjikitile, living at Ngarambe, declared that by sprinkling people with water he could give them complete immunity against the German bullets and they would be able to drive away the foreigners from their land. His messengers carried the water throughout southern Tanganyika. Although the Germans were initially defeated, fresh reinforcements were rushed to the area to quell the revolt. The Africans, armed only with spears, bows and arrows, were no match for the machine guns and rifles of the German soldiers. The water did not protect them from the bullets. The Africans confronted the Germans in a pitched battle, and they died in their hundreds. At the battle of Umereka, the Ngoni suffered heavy casualties and some of their leaders got killed.

On 30th August 1905, about 8,000 men of the Mbuga and Pogoro tribes, armed with spears, attacked Mahenge Fort but suffered many casualties and failed to carry away the machine guns that they had captured. In the East, the Ngindo fought a big guerrilla war until their leader, Dubulla Mpanda, was shot in January 1907.

The Germans used the scorched-earth policy, destroying anything they came across and leaving a trail of destruction behind them. Famine broke out and this greatly weakened the Africans. The last blow to the Maji Maji rebellion was the death of the Ngindo leader who had, for a long time, engaged the German forces in guerrilla warfare. His death marked the end of the Maji Maji rebellion.

The effects of Maji Maji

- All over the country about 75,000 Africans died because of war and famine.

- There was a very serious famine which ushered in a period called *Fugafuga*, during which the Africans resorted to eating insects.

- Very many villages were devastated as a result of the scorched-earth policy pursued by the Germans.

- The rebellion led to destruction and the disruption of agricultural life among the people in southern Tanganyika.

- It taught Africans a lesson. They realised that it was futile to fight and that peaceful means should be sought to solve their problems.

- It led to terrible human suffering as many orphans were left behind without anybody to care for them.

- Badly shaken by the revolt, the German government had to reconsider its attitude towards the local people.

- The Germans realised that Africans had the capacity to think, contrary to the racial prejudices of that time.

- A new Governor was appointed to replace Wissman. His name was Rechenberg and he was meant to see to it that no revolt occurred again.

- The use of corporal punishment was abolished.

- The settlers' demand for forced labour was curbed.

- Africans were encouraged, in less coercive ways, to grow cash crops.

- The officers or akidas who had misbehaved were demoted or sacked.

- Africans also learnt that organised leadership was necessary in any campaign against oppressive rule.

- Forced labour was abolished.

Revision 24

1 (a) How did the Germans administer Tanganyika up to 1914?

(b) What changes did the British introduce in their administration after the Germans up to 1939?

2 (a) Explain the Anglo-German conflicts in East Africa between 1886 and 1890.

(b) How were these conflicts solved by 1890?

3 (a) Why did the Maji Maji uprising occur?

(b) Describe the cause of the struggle with the colonisers.

(c) What were the effects of the uprising?

4   Describe the German system of administration of Tanganyika between 1919 and 1939.

5   (a)   How did Germany gain control of Tanganyika between 1884 and 1890?

    (b)   Describe the German system of administration in Tanganyika before 1914.

25

The First World War and its effects

The First World War began in August 1914 between Germany and Austria and their allies on one side, and Britain, France, Russia and their allies on the other. This war was a struggle to control Europe, but in the end it spread all over the world. Since Britian, France and Germany were the leading colonial powers, fighting also took place in their colonies. In 1917, America joined the war, fighting against the German side.

Britain hoped that their colonies would remain neutral and troops would only be sent if Germany attacked British territories. However, the Germans knew of Britain's plans and decided to cause trouble in Britain's overseas territories.

At the beginning of the war, the German army in East Africa consisted of about 2,750 soldiers while Britain had 4,250 soldiers. German civilians quickly joined the army and Britain recruited many Africans into its army. Soon the British army outnumbered the German army by almost 2:1.

How the war was fought in East Africa

The British navy attacked Dar-es-Salaam and Tanga. The German army led by General Lettow von Vorbeck, moved into the Kilimanjaro area to attack the Uganda Railway. When fresh British troops arrived from India, the British mounted an attack on Tanga but were repulsed. In 1915 attacks were made on German posts round Lake Victoria. It is worth noting that the British had complete control over the coastal waters and they stopped supplies from reaching the Germans.

General J.C. Smuts came from South Africa and forced the Germans out of the mountain area to the River Ruvu region. Although the Germans were sickly and hungry, they would not surrender. Yet more and more British–led troops kept coming in to try and drive the Germans out of East Africa. General Edward Northey came from Rhodesia. The Belgian army, on the other hand, occupied Rwanda.

Throughout 1917, the Germans engaged in many battles against their enemies but at the end of that year, they were forced out of East Africa. Thereafter General Lettow von Vorbeck invaded Mozambique and northern Rhodesia. The First World War was brought to an end in 1918 when the Germans and their allies surrendered to Britain.

Effects of the First World War in East Africa
The war, which lasted from 1914 to 1918, had far-reaching economic, political and social effects on the peoples of East Africa.

- The war completely devastated the economies of East Africa. Furthermore, European farms and plantations were abandoned and neglected.

- In many areas, African farms suffered equally badly. Consequently, there was serious famine.

- Very many people suffered from diseases such as influenza.

- Large numbers of troops, on both sides, were killed or wounded. The majority of these were Africans.

- The war also ended the impression among Africans that the Europeans were neither vulnerable to bullets nor cowards.

- Germany was forced to surrender all her overseas territories to the League of Nations.

- The nations responsible for the mandated territories were instructed to pay attention to the economic, social and moral welfare of the inhabitants and to submit annual progress reports.

- German East Africa was taken over by the British and it was renamed Tanganyika in 1920.

- In 1929 Sir Horace Byatt became Governor of Tanganyika and a four-member Executive Council was set up to advise him.

- The German plantations were taken over by British settlers.

26

Economic and social development of Tanganyika (1900 - 1963)

The economic development of Tanganyika took off in 1900 when many settlers came to the country to open plantations. They were helped by a steady supply of forced labour. This enabled the government to develop both African cash crop farming and settler agriculture.

In 1902, the government founded a biological and agricultural college. Experiments were done on soils, crops, fertilisers and plant diseases. In the same year, the settlers started commercial farming in the Dar-es-Salaam area. The settlers also embarked on cotton growing around Usukuma. In 1905, the government set up a centre in Mpangariya in the Rufiji valley to show Africans how to grow cotton.

Africans were also encouraged to grow coconuts. Sisal growing was left to the settlers. Sisal was imported from Florida in 1892 and fortunately the climate and the soil of Tanganyika proved ideal for it. Sisal production was stimulated by the rise in world sisal prices. By 1906 sisal was earning Tanganyika 1,268,000 Marks annually, and by 1912 it was earning 7,359,000 Marks.

Coffee growing was started in Usambara in the 1890s but it did not do well owing to poor soil conditions. Around 1912, the settlers and Africans started growing coffee in the Bukoba and Kilimanjaro areas.

Though there was a lot of resistance to cotton, by 1914 it was being grown successfully by the Wasukuma in Mwanza and in parts of the Rufiji valley. The growing of rubber trees was encouraged in Morogoro and Tanga districts but this was abandoned when the world price fell drastically in 1913.

Transport and trade

If the First World War had not displaced the Germans, Tanganyika would have developed at a faster rate than either Kenya or Uganda. According to the Germans, a vast country like Tanganyika with such abundant natural resources, could not be economically beneficial to Germany without the existence of an elaborate network of roads and railways. The first railway to be built in Tanganyika ran from Tanga to Moshi. Its construction started at Tanga in 1893, it reached Mombo in 1905, and it was extended to Moshi in 1912. This line was of great importance to the settlers in Usumbara because it enabled them to transport their products to Tanga.

The central railway line was started at Dar-es-Salaam in 1905, it reached Tabora in 1912, and it was extended to Kigoma in 1914. New areas for agriculture were therefore opened up around Morogoro and Tabora where sisal production yielded a lot of profit for the farmers. The Indians were then encouraged to move into Tanganyika to engage in trade. The largest of the Indian concerns was that of Allidina Visram.

Development of education and towns up to 1914

Educational work was taken up by the missionaries who built many schools. By 1914, the missionaries had set up 1832 schools. But the German government also set up schools and by the time the British took over Tanganyika, there were 83 academic and 6 technical schools. Unfortunately, the outbreak of World War I halted educational progress in Tanganyika.

The Germans were great town builders. The towns were administrative, military and cultural centres. Dar-es-Salaam became the capital of Tanganyika. Around 1889, Dar-es-Salaam was a small Arab town with only 350 people, but by 1905 it had become a well planned port with wide streets, stone buildings and 24,000 inhabitants.

Since the Germans believed that the sudden abolition of slave trade would disrupt the traditional economic patterns, they stopped it gradually. When the British took over Tanganyika the slave trade had already been abolished.

Before 1945

Sir Horace Byatt, the first British Governor to be appointed after the departure of the Germans from Tanganyika, was pro-African. He discouraged the settlers from coming to Tanganyika in very large numbers. Furthermore, the Land Ordinance of 1923 strictly regulated land allocation to the white settlers. They could only acquire land on a leasehold basis. Otherwise the land which the Germans had acquired before the First World War was given to Africans.

When Cameron took over the administration of Tanganyika from Byatt, he encouraged the Europeans to farm in the territory as an example to African farmers. The production of cash crops went up rapidly and sisal output increased from 20,834 tons in 1913 to 45,828 tons in 1929. Coffee production also increased from 1,059 tons in 1913 to 10,000 tons in 1928.

All these increases in the production of cash crops were mainly due to improvements in transport. A rail link between Tabora and Mwanza was completed in 1928 and another from Moshi to Arusha the following year. Gold was discovered in Mwanza and Musoma districts and its production increased steadily. Gold became one of the most important exports of the country.

It is worth noting that the economy of Tanganyika improved a lot in the 1920s. British grants-in-aid to Tanganyika rose from £408,109 in 1922 to £3,085,891 in 1926. By 1926, Tanganyika had a balanced budget so it did not need any financial assistance from outside. Increased agricultural production enabled people to meet their tax obligations. In 1930 the collection of both hut and poll taxes amounted to £750,000. In addition to this, a duty tax was imposed on certain imports.

Tanganyika was already forging ahead when it was hit hard by the economic depression of 1929-33. The world depression was caused by a serious economic crisis in America. In the 1920s almost all countries in the world relied on America for financial help but, in 1929, there was an economic crisis which led to the collapse of world trade. This collapse was termed 'The Great Depression'. It lasted until 1933. The countries which suffered most during the depression were those whose economies depended on the sale of raw materials.

The depression brought about a slump in Tanganyika's exports and this seriously affected the farmers, especially plantation owners. In order to offset the effects of this economic depression, the government encouraged more immigrants and advised farmers to grow more food. With food available in sufficient quantities, Tanganyika managed to go through the depression. By 1933, the budget was balancing once again.

Tea and sugar had been tried and they had proved successful. To speed up recovery new land was made available for the settlers. In 1938 a Labour Advisory Board was set up to handle complaints by workers on the settlers' farms about poor pay. Unfortunately, World War Two interrupted Tanganyika's economic development which, however, resumed immediately after the war in 1945.

After 1945

After the Second World War, Tanganyika, like other British colonies such as Uganda and Kenya, started to develop industries. The processing industries were most important at that time. Tanganyika processed tobacco in Dar-es-Salaam to make cigarettes. Cotton processing industries were also put up at Mwanza and Dar-es-Salaam. Clothes were manufactured from the cotton at Mwanza and Dar-es-Salaam. Sugar factories were set up in Arusha and Chini, south of Moshi, and at Chamilil and Muhoroni.

In addition to the above industries, Tanganyika also manufactured soap and margarine out of cotton seeds. Wheat, maize and rice were grown in many places and industries were also set up to process those cereals.

The tourist industry was also started. Tanganyika possessed some natural attractions. In 1948, the East African Tourist Association requested the British Overseas Airways Corporation (BOAC) to bring tourists to East Africa including Tanganyika. By the time it got its independence Tanganyika was quite sound economically. A national bank was established to handle financial transactions and to provide credit to traders and upcoming industrialists.

Education before 1945

As we have already seen, by 1914 education in Tanganyika was already making progress. In 1920, the British government appointed a Director of Education, and by 1928 many schools had been established. Many of the schools were established in eight provinces out of the eleven in the territory. The work of the Director brought a lot of improvement. In 1934 about two types of schools were already in existence in Tanganyika. These were elementary schools and middle schools.

Elementary schools

These consisted of:

(a) mission schools which usually had untrained staff and concentrated on the teaching of religion,

(b) government village schools staffed by teacher employees of the Department of Education, and

(c) mission schools which were aided by the government. These schools employed trained teachers and they taught the government syllabus.

In all these schools Kiswahili was the medium of instruction.

Middle schools

The middle schools were government-owned. English was the medium of communication and instruction. The Education Department prepared terminal examinations at the end of Standard Five and awarded certificates. Secondary education was not provided at that time.

Education after 1945

Little was done to improve the system of education before Tanganyika gained independence in 1961. Immediately Tanganyika gained independence, the education system was transformed. A single system of government schools was put in place to replace the old one. Local authorities were given the responsibility for primary schools.

Meanwhile, the Ministry of Education was empowered to set up Boards of Governors for post-primary institutions. The ministry was also empowered to revise the rules concerning grants-in-aid, to register teachers and to approve the owners and managers of schools.

The establishment of the single system of education had an immediate effect on the educational standards in Tanganyika. The number of Higher School Certificate candidates increased from 168 in 1961 to 624 in 1964, and the number of School Certificate candidates increased from 1398 in 1961 to 3955 in 1964.

Furthermore, teacher training colleges were set up to absorb post-primary school graduates. The primary course was extended from four years to eight years. A technical school was set up in Dar-es-Salaam and additional technical facilities were made available.

All schools were meant to admit students without any discrimination on the basis of sex, colour or race. In all the schools, English was encouraged as the medium of instruction.

Revisions 25 & 26

1 (a) Why was East Africa involved in World War I?

   (b) What were the effects of the war on the peoples of East Africa?

2 (a) How did East Africa get involved in World War I?

   (b) What were the effects of this war on East Africa?

3 (a) Describe the development of cash crops in Tanganyika between 1900 - 1945.

   (b) What were the effects of this development on Tanganyika?

4 Describe the development of education in Tanganyika during the colonial period.

5 Describe the development of:-

(a) agriculture and

(b) communications in Tanganyika from the end of World War I up to the country's independence.

27

Economic and social development of Uganda (1900-63)

Economic development in Uganda before 1920

The British colonialists, like the Germans, wanted their colonies to pay for their administration. In order to do so, it was important to develop agriculture to generate money and increase tax revenues. Since Uganda's economy was basically subsistence, small - scale farmers were the cornerstone of agricultural development.When Uganda was declared a British protectorate in 1894, efforts were made to tap Uganda's economic potential.

By 1900, the economy of Uganda was still dependent on the export of ivory, hides and chillies. The only way to diversify the economy, so as to reduce the burden on the British taxpayers who shouldered colonialist administrative costs, was to introduce cash crops in Uganda. Therefore, the main task of British colonial authorities in Uganda was to convince the farmers to adopt new methods of farming and to grow the new crops.

A Scientific and Forestry Department was set up to help the farmers. People were encouraged to plant trial crops such as coffee, wheat, sugar cane, groundnuts, rubber, chillies, tea, cotton, vanilla and cocoa. Initially, however, it was only cotton which proved successful as a cash crop.

Cotton was already growing wild in Uganda. But it was introduced as a commercial crop in 1904 by K. Borup of the Uganda Company. Cotton seeds were distributed in Buganda, Busoga, Ankole and Bunyoro. The crop became very important and, just three years after the distribution of the seeds, its export revenue had risen to £52,000. By that time, it had become the leading export of the country. Eastern Uganda quickly overtook Buganda as the leading producer of cotton in the country.

The cotton seeds supplied for planting were, however, of many different types. This was a problem to the farmers as the different varieties of seed yielded cotton of variable quality. When the 1908 Cotton Ordinance was passed, it gave the Governor a wide range of powers to standardise the quality of cotton in Uganda. He ordered the destruction of all cotton seeds except the American Upland type which yielded very high quality cotton.

Another problem that the farmers faced was ginning their cotton. This was also solved by the 1908 Cotton Ordinance. The Governor banned hand-ginning in order to ensure the production of clean and properly graded cotton. Three important ginneries were opened to handle all the cotton in Uganda.

The production of cotton on a small scale was seen as profitable to both the individual farmers in Uganda as well as to the protectorate. Other crops which were tried out were coffee, simsim, rubber, sugar cane and groundnuts. Coffee proved to be very successful. By 1914, there were about 130 coffee plantations in Uganda. In Bugisu the Arabica type was grown on Mount Elgon.

To tackle the problem of transport, Sir Hesketh Bell encouraged the importation of vehicles and bicycles. He also embarked on an extensive programme of road building, including all-weather roads, to link the main centres of southern Uganda.

However, there was not enough money to finish the construction of roads. Many areas were still unconnected and the ox-cart and head porterage remained the only means of transport. Still, compared to Kenya and Tanzania, Uganda had the best roads by 1912. A rail link was built between Kampala and Port Bell on Lake Victoria. Another railway line was started further east. This was the Jinja - Namasagali line which was built to serve the cotton growers of Busoga. All imports and exports at that time had to cross Lake Victoria by steamer to Kisumu. Trading centres grew rapidly around local and central headquarters of colonial administration and around communication lines. The centres gradually developed into towns.

Sir Hesketh Bell

The Asians, whose traditional occupation is trade, opened shops in many trading centres in Uganda. Prominent among them was Allidina Visram. He was the first Indian to open a shop in Kampala. Within a short time, he had set up a soda factory, a cotton ginnery, workshops and mills.

The Indians controlled trade in Uganda. They bought produce from the Africans, lent money and imported the goods needed by the Europeans as well as the Africans.

Health

Before the First World War, people in Uganda died in large numbers from sleeping sickness, mainly around the Lake Victoria area. The disease was traced to the tsetse fly. Immediately, an order was issued to the people living around the tsetse fly breeding grounds near Lake Victoria to evacuate the area. With the help of Sir Apollo Kagwa, people were resettled in tsetse fly free areas and the death rate drastically declined.

Other rampant diseases at this time were syphilis, small pox, meningitis and influenza. Although the colonialists had very limited funds at that time, their efforts saved many lives.

Economic development before 1945

From 1920 to 1945, some economic development, especially in agriculture, was registered. The production of cotton and coffee continued to be based on peasant cultivation. Sugar was grown on a commercial basis only from around 1920 by Nanji Kalidas Mehta, one of the leading Indian entrepreneurs in Uganda. He acquired about 2000 acres of land and set up a plantation at Lugazi, in eastern Buganda. He also built a factory which produced refined sugar. Another sugar cane plantation was set up by Madhvani at Kakira near Jinja.

Sugar production picked up quickly since it had a ready market within the country. Tea and tobacco production started in the 1930s but they were grown on small areas of land. The Africans took the production of these crops seriously and, by 1945, tobacco had become the third major export from Uganda. Minerals were also explored and in 1925 copper proved to be of great importance.

A development commission was set up in 1920 and it recommended that plantation agriculture by settlers be encouraged. The commission also wanted Africans discouraged from growing cotton so that they could provide labour on the European plantations, but the Colonial Office rejected that recommendation.

The Great Depression of 1929-33 also affected Uganda. Its exports fell from £4,000,000 to £2,000,000 in 1930 and the country became indebted to the tune of £230,000. But by 1936, the country had recovered. From the financial point of view, an African farmer in Uganda was better off than his counterparts in Kenya and Tanzania. He was able to educate his children, and to buy the necessities of life.

Commerce and trade were mainly in the hands of Indians and Europeans. These middlemen deliberately fixed very low prices for African crops. They routinely ignored complaints from the farmers. Improvements in transport and communications continued. By 1932, there were 2900 kilometres of good main roads in Uganda.

In 1931, a branch line of the Uganda Railway was constructed from Tororo to Soroti via Mbale. In the same year, a new railway track from Jinja to Kampala across the River Nile was opened. Later in 1948, a line was constructed from Kampala to the western part of Uganda.

Between 1946 and 1963

There was a great increase in the demand for Ugandan products after the Second World War. In 1956, the western railway line was extended to Kilembe. A long northern line was built from Soroti to Gulu and on to Pakwach. Tarmacking of some of the major roads was also in progress.

The Uganda Development Corporation was formed to finance new projects and also to encourage tourists. In 1953, the corporation joined the Commonwealth Development Corporation to finance the Kilembe copper mines.

A hydroelectric power station was opened at the Owen Falls Dam in 1954. This encouraged the growth of industries set up by local businessmen and foreign companies. Industrial products included cigarettes, cloth, blankets, soft drinks, cement, beer, frozen fish, shoes and matches.

By 1962, Uganda had made much progress economically, with exports worth about £39,200,000. The government worked very hard to diversify the economy by establishing industries, especially in Kampala and Jinja, and encouraging peasants to grow a variety of crops.

Education

In Uganda, formal education was first introduced by the Arabs to spread Islam, their religion. They set up Koranic schools. Later, the missionaries introduced Western education. The colonial government did not interfere in the education imparted to the Africans until 1922.

Bishop Tucker was one of the prominent missionaries who pioneered the development of education in Uganda. In 1893, he opened a training college at Mukono for Anglican Protestants. The first schools were meant for the sons of chiefs although some children of ordinary people were also enrolled in Catholic-run schools. Until the 1920s, all the schools in Uganda were owned and run by Catholic and Anglican missionaries.

Namilyango School was opened in 1902 by the Mill Hill Fathers. By 1902 the White Fathers had opened about twenty-three primary schools in their missions in Uganda. Mengo High School was opened by the Church Missionary Society in 1903. This was followed by Budo in 1906, then Kisubi and

Gayaza. All these schools emphasised the teaching of Bible knowledge, the reading of English books, geography and mathematics.

Before 1922, the government only gave small grants to the mission schools. Under Governor Geoffrey Archer (1922-25), the colonial government started to take the lead in education. In 1922, a technical school was opened at Makerere. Later it became a technical training school. Grants to mission schools greatly increased from 1923 onwards.

However, the mission schools had a number of weaknesses:

- The kind of education provided at the mission schools was more literary than practical, and the educational activities conducted there were not at all relevant to African needs.

- Agricultural education was ignored despite the agricultural skills needed to exploit Uganda's great agricultural potential.

- Alexander Mackay had embarked on industrial training but this was ignored by the mission schools.

- Hygiene, health and animal husbandry were not taught either.

- There was lack of trained teachers. The sub-grade teachers provided inadequate and sub-standard instruction.

- But the root cause of all the above weaknesses lay in the fact that the protectorate government had not established a Department of Education.

However in 1923, the Duke of Devonshire, the then Colonial Secretary, set up an Advisory Committee on Native Education in British Tropical Africa under Phelps-Stokes.

Phelps-Stokes Commission

This commission did a commendable job in Uganda. Their work soon altered the education system which hitherto had predominantly been run by the missionaries. They commended the missionaries for the good work done despite the fact that they had very limited funds. The commission made the following recommendations:

(i) The appointment of a Director of Education to conduct a careful and systematic survey of the existing organisations and their methods and to supervise the school system all over the country.

(ii) The Advisory Board, which had been appointed some years before, should represent government missions, settlers and the native people.

(iii) The government should increase financial support to education, and the Department of Education and the Advisory Board guarantee effective use of such support.

(iv) The government should supervise and administer schools through the Director of Education, inspectors and the Advisory board.

(v) Agriculture, Physical Science, Nature Study, health and industrial training should be included in the school curriculum.

(vi) English should be used as a lingua franca for Uganda besides Luganda.

(vii) The schools in Uganda should be renamed and the standards of Budo, Namilyango and Kisubi should be improved to enable their students to satisfy the entry requirements for Makerere Technical School or for theological colleges.

The government implemented the recommendations of the Phelps-Stokes Commission to improve the education system in Uganda. A Director of Education was appointed in 1924. He was Eric Hussey who had been working in Sudan. He found that the village mission schools were many but poorly staffed. The government could not fund them all owing to lack of funds. He therefore selected only fifty schools to be funded and managed by government even though they still belonged to the missionaries. Hussey also established provincial and district education boards. All these boards were chaired by administrative officers.

Hussey started many technical schools. From the outset, Makerere offered a medical course in 1922. In 1926, a junior secondary teacher's course was also introduced. In 1928, Mulago was already a big hospital with a medical school and the first medical assistants were trained there the same year. In 1927, Namilyango, Buddo and Kisubi were turned into secondary schools.

The first schoolmasters' class, Makerere University (1925 – 1927)

Education between 1930 and 1945

The number of schools increased tremendously in this period. Busoga college was opened in 1909 but was transferred to Mwiri in 1933. That same year, Makerere launched a course leading to the Cambridge School Certificate. In 1935, five out of six students passed the Cambridge School Certificate examination. In 1936, the Advisory Board requested that every District Board had to have at least one woman member. Many junior secondary schools were upgraded to the Cambridge School Certificate standard and, in the same year, a woman Director of Education was appointed.

Sir Philip Mitchell, the Governor of Uganda between 1935 and 1940, was keen on the development of higher education.

Makerere was promoted to a full university college in 1950 and in 1961 it ceased to be a university college but gained the full autonomous status of a university. In order to meet the enrolment needs of Makerere College, many vocational schools were converted to secondary schools and the school enrolment rose from 226 in 1935 to 1335 in 1939. The number of full primary schools also rose from 23 to 78 in the same period.

Between 1945 and 1962
Educational progress was slow in Uganda from 1945 to 1962. Dr Worthington, who was an administrator, drew up a ten-year programme whose aim was to increase economic production rather than expand social services.

However, A.B. Cohen, who succeeded Worthington, knew that economic development without political and social advancement was impossible. He therefore appointed a commission of inquiry under de Bunsen, the Principal of Makerere, to investigate the state of education in the country and submit proposals for its future organisation and development. The de Bunsen recommendations were adopted and used until 1962 when Uganda achieved its independence.

Makerere University Main Hall

28

Economic and social development of Kenya (1900 - 1963)

Kenya was declared a British protectorate in July 1895, partly because the British wanted to secure a safe route to Uganda. The construction of the Uganda Railway was therefore a turning point in the economic development of Kenya. The Asians who participated in the construction of the railway stayed on and, as traders, they played a crucial role in the economic development of the colony.

In 1902, Sir Charles Eliot, the British Commissioner, was given powers by the Crown Land Ordinance to sell, grant or to lease unoccupied land. This scheme greatly increased the number of white settlers in Kenya.

African farming was encouraged. Nyanza was considered a suitable area for cotton production, but when the crop was introduced there in 1906, it failed. The Africans continued with the production of simsim, groundnuts and maize. The export of those crops increased between 1907 and 1914.

By 1919, the Africans were producing more of the crops than the white settlers. The settlers had a very hard life at the beginning. Clearing bushes was an uphill task because labour was scarce since the Africans were contented with their subsistence way of life. They also had to discover the right crops to grow through trial and error. However, the white settlers soon made an important contribution towards the economic development of Kenya.

- They conducted experiments on wheat and other crops like potatoes, which became very important in the colony.

- They set up large-scale farms on which a large number of Africans were employed.

- Through their experiments, they introduced scientific stock-rearing. This was done on Lord Delamere's Equator Ranch at Njoro. These experiments encouraged the government to set up an experimental stock farm at Naivasha.

- Coffee, which was introduced in Kenya by the Roman Catholic missionaries near Nairobi in 1899, was first grown on a large scale by the white settlers.

Farmers quickly established new coffee plantations when the world price of coffee rose in 1910. By 1920, coffee had become the protectorate's most important export crop.

Economic development of Kenya between 1920 and 1945

Kenya was seriously hit by the economic slump of 1920-21. This slump came after the First World War. The government of Kenya responded to the situation by encouraging maize growing. It also passed a law prohibiting the importation of wheat, meat and dairy products into Kenya. This law increased demand for those products within the country. Railway freight charges were also cut to facilitate the transportation and sale of farmers' products.

The economy of Kenya then picked up and prospered greatly between 1922-29. National revenue rose from £1.64 million in 1922 to £3.33 million in 1929. Within that period, the expenditure on public works increased from £206,000 to £520,000. During the same period, the railway network was extended from Nakuru to Eldoret and Kitale to serve fertile farming areas.

A westward line was extended from Eldoret to Uganda. Other extensions were built to Nyeri, Nanyuki, Thomson's Falls and Solai and the line from Voi to Taveta was improved. The Kenya highlands were therefore well served with a railway transport network. In addition, deep water berths were constructed at Mombasa Harbour.

The economic depression of 1929-33 hurt the farmers badly. They lost money when the value of produce fell. The areas under cultivation dropped from 644,000 acres in 1930 to 502,000 acres in 1936. The depression also led to a sharp decline in revenue for a government which was already heavily indebted.

Kenya remained a predominately agricultural country with agro-based industries up to 1945. The exploitation of soda, gold deposits and forests did not increase. The Second World War, which broke out in 1939, created a new political consciousness among the Kenyans, which led eventually to the attainment of independence in 1963.

Between 1945 and 1963

After the Second World War, the economy of Kenya picked up quite fast. Secondary industries grew. While most of them were agricultural processing industries, there were a growing number of manufacturing industries producing consumer goods for everyday use.

Kenya's market beyond its borders grew rapidly and, in 1954, the value of its exports to its neighbours exceeded £3 million. Agricultural production also increased tremendously. Butter, cheese and milk were processed and marketed inside and outside the country by Kenya Creameries.

Meat was obtained from the uplands and flour, jam, soft drinks and canned fruit from the Kenya Farmers' Association.

By 1963, Kenya was already producing corrugated iron-sheets, as well as products such as blankets, buttons, prefabricated building materials, cooking pots, mugs, knives, bottles and matches.

Education in Kenya

Education in Kenya was left in the hands of the missionaries who established about forty main mission schools, in which the teaching of Bible knowledge was of paramount importance. A Department of Education was later established and the government started to direct its attention towards the education of Africans in 1911. The first government school for Africans was opened in 1915. This was meant to train teachers and also to provide technical courses. The government paid grants to this school. A capitation grant of £5 per year per student for exams was maintained up to 1919. By the 1920s, the Africans were already rating education highly because they considered it a gateway to material wealth. They also looked at education as an opportunity to articulate grievances and to challenge settler domination.

In the mission schools, the courses offered were purely academic and European in content. This changed when the Phelps-Stokes Commission of 1924 recommended that agricultural and practical courses be offered to Africans. This led to the opening of a Jeanes school at Kabete for training supervisors for local schools in 1925.

Kenya was divided into school areas and in each of the areas a separate educational system was set up for European, Asian and African children. Government assisted and also licensed both private and government schools. In addition to these responsibilities, the government agreed to pay four-fifths of European staff salaries and two-thirds of the African staff salaries. It also agreed to meet half of the cost of building and equipping the schools as well as meeting the boarding and upkeep fees of students.

In 1926, the main Protestant missions combined to found Alliance High School which became the first secondary school for Africans in the country. The Holy Ghost Fathers also developed a school similar to Alliance High School at Kabaa and the CMS built another one at Maseno.

In 1931 an Education Ordinance set up School Area Committees. Subsequently, the Education Ordinance of 1934 introduced District Education Boards. These boards were manned by representatives of local native councils, government and missions. The schools set up at this time included village, central and secondary schools. There were also some few industrial schools and teacher training colleges. Secondary schools were opened in Maseno and Yala in 1938 and 1939 respectively.

Education between 1945 and 1963

After the Second World War, primary education was left in the hands of local councils. Teachers, both in grant-aided and in government schools, received the same salaries. When secondary schools expanded after the war, a committee was set up to examine and report on the curriculum scope, content as well as the teaching methods used in the African education system. The committee recommended that:

(i)   The District Education Boards should be responsible for primary and intermediate education, but the grants should come from the central government.

(ii) 2000 primary schools should be set up in Kenya by 1961.

(iii) A unified Teaching Service should be set up and the Education Department should be adequately staffed.

(iv) Grades should be set for teachers. A student had to hold a school certificate in order to take a Diploma in Education.

In 1963, the Royal College of Nairobi became a university college and together with Makerere and Dar-es-Salam constituted the University of East Africa.

Revision 27 & 28

1   (a   Describe the development of cash crops in Uganda between 1900 and 1963.

    (b)   What were the effects of this development on Tanganyika?

2   Describe the development of education in Uganda during the colonial period.

3   Describe the development in communication between 1900 and 1962 in Uganda.

4   (a)   Explain the developments in education in Uganda during the period 1900 - 1920.

    (b)   Why did the government become interested in controlling education after 1920?

5 (a) Describe the development of cash crops in Kenya between 1900 and 1945.

(b) What were the effects of this development for Kenya?

6 Describe the development of education in Kenya during the colonial period.

7 Describe the development of communication between 1900 and 1960 in Kenya.

8 (a) Why did Kenya develop as a settler colony?

(b) Why did the settlers send a combined Asian and European delegation to the Colonial Secretary in 1923?

29

Uganda's constitutional development (1906 - 1963)

The constitutional development of Uganda owes a lot to the motives behind the partition of East Africa by the British. One of those motives was to exploit the natural resources of Uganda. Since the motives were more economic than political, constitutional development in Uganda was slower than in Kenya and Tanganyika. Constitutional development in Uganda started in 1900 when the Buganda Agreement was signed.

According to an Order-in-Council of 1902, Uganda was to be governed by a Commissioner. This was however changed in 1907 when the title of Commissioner was replaced with Governor.

At the request of the European settlers in Uganda, a legislative council was established by Sir Robert Coryndon in 1919. The Legislative Council (Legco) consisted of the Governor, four official and three unofficial members, two Europeans and one Asian. But the Asians continued to agitate for equal representation, until it was granted in 1933. Africans were not directly represented in the Council and Buganda made it clear that it had no interest in that institution.

Sir Philip Mitchell, the Governor of Uganda between 1935 and 1940, attempted to enlarge the Council to include all the various interest groups in Uganda but failed. The outbreak of the Second World War brought constitutional development in Uganda to a halt.

Immediately after the Second World War, there was a constitutional crisis in Uganda. There were no political parties and the Baganda felt that there was no need for a Legislative Council. Yet they felt that they were not fairly represented in the Lukiiko and they also suspected that attainment of independence would take a very long time. There were therefore many riots in the 1940s. Economic and political discontent increased considerably in Buganda in the 1940s. People wanted more participation in the direction of their affairs through more representation in the Lukiiko. Such discontent found an outlet in the Buganda riots of 1945 and the assassination of Buganda Prime Minister Nsibirwa. Riots engineered by Uganda African Farmers Association occurred in 1949. These were better organised and more complex.

The Africans demanded that they should be allowed to market their crops themselves instead of through the European and Indian middlemen. They also demanded that the Kabaka should democratise the Lukiiko by increasing the representative side to 60 members. This would cater for the interests of the common people.

The Legislative Council was not as important in Uganda between 1941 and 1949 as it was in Kenya and Tanganyika. In order to speed up constitutional advancement in Uganda, the British government expanded the Legco to include other interest groups. In 1945, the first three Africans, mainly from Buganda, eastern and western Uganda were appointed to the Legco. The Lukiiko continued to shun the Legco on the grounds that their participation would undermine the independent status of Buganda.

In 1950, the members of the Legco were doubled to 16. Among them were eight Africans. These included two from Buganda, one of whom was nominated by the Kabaka.

In 1952, Mr A.C. Wallis surveyed local governments throughout the country and recommended some constitutional changes. These recommendations were accepted as a basis for future policy. The implementation of the recommendations led to the exile of the Kabaka in November 1953. This was referred to as the 'Kabaka Crisis'. It also led to the review of the Buganda Agreement in 1954. The review of the Buganda Agreement was done by Sir Keith Hancock and the Baganda leaders. Hancock was a constitutional expert from England. He held several meetings for over a year with the Baganda leaders in order to end the Kabaka crisis. Under the 1955

Agreement, which amended that of 1900, Buganda accepted the following conditions:

Kabaka Mutesa II

(i) The Kabaka became a constitutional monarch with executive powers vested in the Prime Minister (Katikiro).

(ii) All the ministers in the Kabaka's government had to be appointed with the approval of the Governor of Uganda.

(iii) Closer union would only be implemented with popular support from the people.

(iv) Buganda was to remain part of Uganda.

(v) Mutesa II could only return if the Lukiiko invited him back.

(vi) Constitutional changes were not to be effected until several years had elapsed.

(vii) The Lukiiko members were to be elected by the county councils.

Meanwhile, in 1954, membership in the Legco was increased to 56. The following year African membership was increased to 30. The crossbench system was abolished and some of the members sat on the government side of the house. This side had 10 official members, five Ministers, two Parliamentary Secretaries, 13 back-benchers, seven of whom were Africans. On the representative side there were 18 Africans, six Europeans and six Asians. In 1958, there was a proposal for a Speaker to replace the Governor and also some unofficial members to be elected from all regions except Karamoja. This annoyed the Lukiiko and they claimed that this proposal was an abrogation of the Buganda Agreement which stipulated that there should be no constitutional change for seven years.

30

Uganda's political development (1906 - 1962)

After the signing of the 1900 Buganda Agreement and the subsequent signing of agreements with Toro, Ankole and Bunyoro, British rule was gradually extended to other parts of the country. By 1902 the areas west of the Rift Valley had become part of Kenya. In 1912, West Nile was transferred from Sudan to Uganda. In 1911, the Toro-Ankole border was demarcated. Turkana district was transferred from Uganda to Kenya in 1926. Thus, the present borders of Uganda were finally fixed. Entebbe became the administrative headquarters of Uganda while Kampala became the commercial centre.

After the Second World War, Uganda began to experience the influence of nationalist movements and opposition to European colonialism. Unlike Kenya and Tanganyika, from 1906 to 1945 Uganda was in a state of political slumber. The delay in the formation of political parties in Uganda has been attributed to:

- The system of indirect rule which allowed Ugandan Africans to participate in their own local governance and seemingly rendered British colonialism less oppressive than in Kenya, for example.

- The absence of large-scale European settlement unlike the situation then obtaining in Kenya.

- The lack of country-wide common interests and grievances, which meant that political groups like the Bataka were more interested in local issues than in a truly mass nationalist movement.

However, after the Second World War, Uganda woke up from its political slumber. Nationalist movements were formed and they started participating in the affairs of the country.

Reasons for nationalist movements in Uganda

- A big number of Ugandans participated in the Second World War. During the course of the war, the Ugandan soldiers observed a number of things. They observed, for instance, that even the whites could die like people of other races, they could also be cowards, and that they were not respected in other lands. All these broadened their knowledge and created a desire for independence.

- At this time, Uganda's educated elite from Makerere and other institutions of higher learning were becoming politically conscious. Other Ugandans had studied overseas in America and Europe. All those people were opposed to colonial rule.

- The Allied countries which won the war promised, through the Atlantic Charter, freedom to all countries after the war. Those Ugandans who were politically aware expected their freedom. This expectation was further fuelled when India, Pakistan, Ceylon and Burma attained independence.

- The new superpowers – the USA and the Soviet Union – were opposed to the continuation of formal European colonialism and this encouraged the Africans to agitate for independence.

- The founding of the United Nations Organisation and its subsequent denunciation of colonialism motivated the Africans.

- The triumph of communism in Europe encouraged the African nationalist movements to demand freedom.

Because of the above reasons, the Ugandan elite started to transcend regional differences in order to organise an effective nationalist movement, not in terms of regions, for this would not be helpful. For this purpose, they formed political parties to articulate African grievances against colonialism and to struggle for independence.

The development of political parties in Uganda

The first national African political party to be formed in Uganda was the Uganda National Congress (UNC). It was formed in 1952 by Mr. Ignatius Musaazi. He had been a leader of the Federation of Uganda African Farmers. This organisation had taken part in the riots of 1945 and 1949 in Buganda against the Asian monopoly over cotton and coffee processing and marketing.

Aims of the Uganda National Congress

(i) The creation of a multi-racial welfare society under a strong, stable and unified government.

(ii) Upholding the dignity and prestige of hereditary rulers in Uganda.

(iii) The planning of a strong economic system in order to raise the standard of living of Ugandans.

(iv) Stopping the exploitation of man by man by upholding uncompromisingly the principles of democracy.

(v) The use of constitutional means to attain independence.

However, right from the beginning, this party faced a great deal of hostility from the Baganda who thought that the formation of the party was an attempt to undermine the influence of their kingdom. This party was dominated by the Protestant Old Boys of Budo and as a result, it did not appeal to the Catholics. Besides, since it was a predominantly Buganda-based and-led party, its support outside Buganda was limited.

The UNC strongly opposed the deportation and exile of the Kabaka in 1953 and it sent a deputation to London to negotiate the release of the Kabaka. In 1955, some members of UNC broke away and formed the Progressive Party. This party was led by E.K. Mulira. It was dominated by Protestants, prosperous farmers and African businessmen, but by 1958, it had become as weak as UNC.

In 1956, the Democratic Party was founded by Matayo Mugwanya, a former Buganda Chief Justice. DP was largely a Catholic party. The leadership of the party was later taken over by Benedicto Kiwanuka, a lawyer. Meanwhile, the protectorate organised the first direct elections in Uganda in 1958. Only people with property worth at least £1000 were qualified to vote. The Baganda and Bagisu boycotted the elections while Ankole indirectly elected its members to the Legco. The Governor nominated the Bugisu and Ankole representatives.

After the election another party was formed. This was the Uganda People's Union. The party had anti-Buganda sentiments. Although it was the first political party to be led by non-Baganda, this party was confined to the Legislative Council.

The Wild Committee (this was a constitutional committee)
In 1958, Government appointed J.V. Wild to head a committee to plan the organisation of the 1961 elections. The members of the Wild Committee, after moving round the country, recommended the following:

(a) That the eligibility to vote should be as wide as possible.

(b) That the majority of seats be open to elections on a common roll, and

(c) That the number of official members be as small as possible.

The above recommendations were adopted by the Protectorate Government, but the Buganda Lukiiko strongly denounced them and said it would not take part in the elections of 1961.

Meanwhile, the Uganda People's Union (UPU) decided to combine with another splinter group of UNC led by A.M. Obote to form the Uganda People's Congress. Obote became the leader of the new party.

219

A.M. Obote (left) and Jomo Kenyatta

1961 elections

During the elections, DP won 43 seats and UPC won 35. Ben Kiwanuka therefore became leader of the Legislative Council and Obote headed the opposition.

This was disappointing to the Buganda Lukiiko. Consequently on 31th December 1960, the Lukiiko declared Buganda independent. However, this unilateral declaration of Buganda's independence did not yield anything for the Lukiiko and Britain did not recognise it. The Lukiiko now resorted to campaigning for a federal constitution.

In September 1961, a constitutional conference was organised in London. All political groups in the protectorate as well as those from the Kabaka's government were represented. They recommended that:

(a) The leader of Government should be called the Prime Minister.

(b) The Prime Minister should be the executive head of the country, advised by Ministers and answerable to the National Assembly.

Benedicto Kiwanuka

(c) Buganda would remain an integral part of Uganda.

(d) Buganda would enjoy a federal relationship with the rest of the country and would send 21 members, elected by the Lukiiko, to the National Assembly.

(e) The Buganda government would control most internal affairs, including justice.

(f) The rulers of Toro, Ankole and Bunyoro would be granted limited federal powers.

(g) The National Assembly would consist of 82 elected and 9 specially appointed members; and a two-thirds majority would be required to make any constitutional amendments, and the constitution of the kingdoms would not be altered without the kingdoms' consent.

As a result of the above, a group of neo-traditionalists calling itself *Mwoyo Gwa Gwanga* emerged. In 1961, this group developed into a political movement, Kabaka Yekka (KY), which means 'King Only'. The main aim of the KY was to defend the position of the Kabaka. Having supported Buganda's demands at the London constitutional conference, UPC formed an alliance with the KY to fight the 1962 elections in Buganda and Uganda.

On 1st March 1962, Uganda attained internal self-government with Ben Kiwanuka as its first Prime Minister. A general election was held in April 1962. This time UPC and KY decided to form an alliance. DP won 22 seats, UPC 37 and KY 21 Buganda seats. UPC and KY thus defeated DP and formed a coalition government. Obote therefore became the Prime Minister of Uganda when Uganda attained her independence on 9th October 1962. Mutesa II became the President.

31

Tanganyika's constitutional development (1918 - 1961)

Tanganyika fell under German dominion in 1885. It remained a German colony until after the First World War when the British took over. Tanganyika was declared a mandate territory of the League of Nations administered by Britain. After the war, the Germans put more emphasis on the economic development of Tanganyika than on constitutional development. Constitutional development only started in Tanganyika under British administration.

Constitutional development: before 1945

After World War I, the British colonial administrative structure was put in place in Tanganyika. In this structure, the Governor was the executive head of the country, assisted by an Executive Council. By 1920, this council comprised the Governor, Deputy Governor/Chief Secretary, the Attorney General, the Treasurer and the Director of Medical and Sanitary Services.

Positive constitutional development in Tanganyika started during the tenure of Governor Sir Donald Cameron in 1925. He set up a Legislative Council (Legco) in 1926. This council comprised ex-officio members, 7 of whom were nominated and two of whom represented Asian interests. The Africans were not given any seats on this council, since according to Cameron, they were still politically immature.

Cameron instituted indirect rule. He ruled through the local rulers, with little help from akidas. After the departure of Cameron, no constitutional changes took place because the future of Tanganyika was still uncertain. The British feared that the Germans might reassert their claim on the territory. It was prudent to adopt a wait-and-see policy. The outbreak of the Second World War in 1939 froze what constitutional changes were in the pipeline.

Between 1945 and 1961

In 1945, the Governor nominated for the first time two Africans to the Legislative Council. These two Africans were chiefs: Chief Shangali of Moshi, and Chief Adam Makwaia of Shinyanga. After two years, another African was nominated to the Legco. This was Chief Adam Sapi. He was nominated by the Governor in 1947. In April 1948, another African, Juma Mirindadi, a school-master in Dar-es-Salaam, was added to the Legco. A constitutional amendment which enlarged the membership of the Legco to 15 official and 14 nominated unofficial seats was made in 1945. Out of these seats, seven were preserved for Europeans, one of whom was to represent African interests, three for Asians and four for Africans.

After the Second World War, the mandate of the League of Nations in Tanganyika was transferred to the United Nations Organisation (UNO). Tanganyika was put under the UNO Trusteeship Council. This council frequently sent out fact - finding missions to which the Africans presented their grievances.

The Trusteeship mission to Tanganyika recommended that:

(i) The Africans should be allocated seats on the Executive Council.

(ii) The British should ensure that the progress of the Tanganyikan Africans was accelerated.

(iii)Each province should be represented by at least one African in the Legco.

(iv) The Africans should be the majority of the unofficial members of the Legco.

(v) An electoral system should be set up to replace the old one which vested substantial powers in the Governor to nominate members of the Legco.

Another Constitutional Committee was set up in 1949 to review the then constitutional structure of Tanganyika and also to recommend the pattern of future constitutional development. In 1951, a commission of inquiry was set up, which recommended that the Executive consist of 8 official and 5 unofficial members (3 Europeans, 1 Asian and 1 African). The Legco had 15 official and 14 unofficial members (7 Europeans, 4 Africans and 3 Asians).

In 1952, the British government agreed to adopt the recommendations on constitutional development. According to the recommendations there was to be equal representation of the three main groups, an enlarged Legco, and a Speaker to replace the Governor to chair the Legco proceedings. Brigadier WHE Schumpham became the first president of the Legco in 1953. The Local Government Ordinance encouraged the election of town or district councils according to the wishes of the majority. In 1954 the composition of the Executive Council was changed in favour of Africans and the number of the unofficial representation became seven (three Africans, two Europeans and two Asians).

In 1955, the British government adopted a policy of racial parity in the Legco. Each of the three racial groups (Africans, Asians and Europeans) had 10 representatives on the representative side of the Legco.

An election bill was passed by the Legco proposing the holding of Legco elections in 1958. In 1957 ministerial posts were announced: six Ministers were to be drawn from among the unofficial members, of whom four were Africans, 1 Asian and 1 European.

In 1958 Richard Turnbull replaced Sir Edward Twining as Governor of Tanganyika. Turnbull intended to speed up the progress of the Tanganyika people towards independence. In 1959, a commission was set up to consider the future of the Legco and the Executive Council. The commission was headed by Sir Richard Ramage and it recommended a large elected Legco with an African majority. It also recommended a Council of Ministers to replace the Executive Council.

Mwalimu Julius Nyerere

Elections were held in 1960 in accordance with the recommendations of the committee. Fifty-eight candidates were elected unopposed. These included Mwalimu Julius Nyerere. Of the 13 contested seats, the Tanganyika African National Union (TANU) won 12. TANU had received the majority vote and was therefore requested to form a government with Nyerere as Chief Minister. The total number of members of the Legco at the time in the National Assembly was 81, out of whom 52 were Africans, 16 Europeans, 11 Asians, 1 Arab and 1 Goan. Only 10 members were nominated.

A constitutional conference which was held in Dar-es-Salaam recommended that Tanganyika should be given internal self-government on 1st May 1961 and independence on 9 December 1961. On 1st May 1961, Tanganyika attained self-government with Julius Nyerere as its first Prime Minister. This was followed by attainment of independence on 9th December 1961. Power was formally handed over to Julius Nyerere by the Duke of Edinburgh.

32

Political development in Tanganyika (1918-1961)

Unlike Ugandans who were in political slumber for a long time, the people of Tanzania were awakened immediately after the First World War.

After the Maji Maji rebellion which opposed German rule, Tanzania did not experience a lot of nationalist influence until 1924.

The first African nationalist movement to be set up in Tanganyika was the Bukoba Bahaya Union. It was formed in 1924 under the leadership of Klemens Kiiza.

Kiiza was an employee of the government and also worked with the Christian missions in Tanzania.

The union put the following demands to the colonial government:

(a) The right to an academic education.

(b) Reform of the system of indirect rule which was imposed on them by Cameron. The Tanganyikans hated those local, illiterate chiefs who were governing them.

(c) Reform of the land tenure system which was imposed on the people. It was called "Nyarubanja" and was almost similar to the *mailo* land system.

Another nationalist movement was the Kilimanjaro Native Planters Association. This was also formed in the same year by the Bukoba Bahaya Union. It was a Chagga association intended to concern itself with the growing and marketing of coffee.

In 1935, the Usangi Sports and Welfare Club was formed. Its main aim was to promote social and recreational activities. But it had a strong underlying motive of educational and economic self-improvement. All the above associations were led by young, educated Africans who were always at loggerheads with the chiefs.

One of the young educated leaders of the Usangi clubs was Martin Kayamba. He was the son of a school teacher. He received his education at Kiungani, a school which had been established by the University Mission to Central Africa (UMCA).

Kayamba was born in Zanzibar in 1891. He was later employed as a clerk in the Tanga District Office. In 1922, with support from government, he founded the Tanganyika Territory African Civil Service Association.

It was from this association that the Tanganyika African Association (TAA) was formed. The Tanganyika African National Union (TANU) was in turn formed from TAA in 1954.

Political development after 1945

The outbreak of the Second World War in 1939 slowed down the political development of Tanganyika. After the war, however, African nationalism gained a lot of momentum. This was due to the fact that the Africans who participated in the war learnt a lot from other countries. They had travelled and fought alongside the white men and realised that the whites were not superior to them at all. They had also gained some experience from the struggle for independence in Asia, South and West Africa. All these gave the ex-soldiers the confidence to agitate for their freedom and independence.

The most important post-war political development was the decision of Britain to place Tanganyika under United Nations trusteeship in 1947. Part of the deal between the British and the United Nations was that political activity by the Tanzanians be permitted. The Tanzanians were, however, only granted this right in the 1950s.

Another important development was the holding of the 5th Pan-African Congress in Britain in 1945. This congress was attended by Kwame Nkrumah, Leopold Senghor, Kamuzu Banda and Nnamdi Azikiwe. The congress led to the call on

African leaders to organise and pressurise the colonialists to grant them independence.

When Tanganyika fell under the juridiction of the Board of Trusteeship, the move towards independence was quickened. Missions were frequently sent to listen to people's grievances. The reports of these missions urged the British to speed up the move to independence for the people of Tanganyika.

In 1949, Sir Edward Twining, the governor of Tanganyika, set up a commission to recommend the constitutional changes to be made. The commission recommended that the official majority in the Legislative Council be retained and that the unofficial seats be divided equally among the three races, i.e Africans, Indians and Europeans.

The Tanganyika African Association attacked the second recommendation. Furthermore, TAA wanted the number of Africans in the Legco to be more than the number of other races combined.

In 1955, Professor Mackenzie was requested to examine the situation on the ground and make recommendations about parliamentary representation. He supported the equal representation of Africans and other races. He even went ahead to recommend that only three contestants should stand in each constituency. All his proposals came into effect in 1955.

In 1953, Julius Nyerere, a renowned academician who had been trained at Edinburgh University, returned to Tanganyika and was elected president of the Tanganyika African Association (TAA). Owing to his dynamism, TAA was soon transformed into a national political party.

On 7th July 1954, the Tanganyika African Association was re-named the Tanganyika African National Union (TANU). This day was termed "Saba-Saba Day". Later, some members of TANU broke away and formed the African Congress (AC).

The visiting United Nations mission was highly impressed by the plans of TANU and recommended that Tanganyika should become independent.

In 1955, Julius Nyerere addressed the United Nations Organisation and he won a lot of respect and sympathy from the member states of UNO.

In 1957, Julius Nyerere became a member of the Legco, a post which he shortly resigned when his proposal of 'one man one vote' was rejected by the Legco.

In 1958, Sir Richard Turnbull was appointed Governor. Right away he embarked on activities geared towards preparing Tanganyika for independence. He had Sir Richard Ramage appointed chairman of a committee meant to consider the future of the Legislative Council and the Executive Council. The committee recommended the following:

(i) The enlargement of the Legco to 71 elected members.

(ii) Reservation of ten seats for whites.

(iii) Setting up of a Council of Ministers to replace the Executive Council.

(iv) Extension of the right to vote to all literate adults with a minimum annual income of £75.

But TANU felt that the recommendation that only literate people be allowed to vote was unfair since some villages had very large populations of illiterate people. They therefore preferred adult suffrage which means 'one man one vote.' However, Julius Nyerere persuaded his people to accept the proposal since it was a big step forward.

At the end of 1959, the Governor announced that a new government would be formed in 1960. This meant that although the country would not yet be fully independent, it would have control over most of the functions of government. This was really the final stage to independence.

An election was organised in 1960. TANU won seventy out of the seventy-one seats available and Julius Nyerere became the first prime minister of Tanganyika. In 1961, he called for independence and he welcomed people of all races into his government provided they stood for the development of the country. He undertook to Africanise the civil service, introducing a special training scheme to accelerate the changeover.

Ian Macleod, the Colonial Secretary, organised a conference in Dar-es-Salaam in March 1961 to work out the final timetable for independence. On May 1, full internal-self government was granted to the people of Tanganyika. Only foreign affairs, defence and the police force remained in the hands of the British government.

Tanganyika received its independence on 9th December 1961 and Julius Nyerere became the first president of the Republic of Tanganyika.

33

Constitutional development in Kenya (1900 - 1963)

Of the three East African countries, constitutional development began earliest in Kenya. This was due to the presence and the interests of the white settlers there.

Between 1895 and 1905, Kenya did not have any representative assembly. In 1906, the British government allowed the formation of an Executive Council in Kenya. The following year, a Legislative Council was also set up. The Governor nominated eight men to the council. The nominees consisted of six official and two unofficial members. The Asians, who were not represented at all, demanded representation. As a result, in 1909, one Asian was nominated to represent Asian interests. In 1914, the settlers were representated on the War Council, which had been set up following the outbreak of the First World War.

Constitutional development after First World War

In 1919, immediately after the First World War, an ordinance was passed. Under its terms, the composition of the Legislative Council was expanded to cater for the representation of various racial groups in the country. The Council was now to include 10 ex-officio members to represent Arab interests in Kenya. It also included eleven unofficial Europeans exclusively elected by the Europeans in Kenya, and two Indians nominated by the Governor. This disparity in representation led to bitter relations between the white settlers and the Asians. Relations between the two groups only began to improve when the British government issued the Devonshire White Paper in 1923. Up to this time the Africans were not represented at alls.

Main points of Devonshire White Paper

(i) Kenya was declared to be primarily an African country and the interests of Africans were declared to be paramount.

(ii) The highlands of Kenya were reserved for European settlement.

(iii) There was to be no racial segregation in residential areas, especially in towns, and no restriction on Indian immigration into Kenya.

(iv) The European demand for self-government in Kenya was dismissed.

(v) The British remained responsible for Kenya.

(vi) The Indians were allowed to elect five members to the Legislative Council.

(vii) African interests were to be represented by Dr Arthur, a prominent missionary in Kenya.

(viii) No further constitutional privileges were promised to the white settlers.

The Devonshire White Paper was a turning point in both the constitutional and political development of Kenya. It left the Europeans and Indians unhappy, but it also laid a firm foundation for the African leaders to articulate their aspirations. The Devonshire White Paper disappointed the Indians deeply and they at first refused to take up the seats reserved for them in the Legco. In 1927, however, they elected one member of their community to the Legco. They only took up all their five seats later, i.e in 1933.

Though the Africans were nominally represented in the Legco in 1931, it was not until 1944 that an African was nominated to the Legco. He was called Mr Eliud Mathu. This concession was partly in response to the formation of the Kenya African Union (KAU), a political party whose goal was to articulate African grievances and promote African aspirations.

Constitutional development after Second World War

In 1946, the white missionary who was representing African interests was replaced by an African. In 1944, the first African, Eliud Mathu, was nominated to the Legislative Council. Mathu was followed by another African, B.A. Changa. In 1946 Changa replaced a missionary who had been nominated to represent African interests in the Legislative Council. The number of African representatives was increased to four in 1948, but this was considered by the Kenya African Union as inadequate. The demand of the Kenya white settlers to have self-government under their dominion only added insult to injury. This was followed by the nomination of four Africans to the Legco in 1948. In 1952, Eliud Mathu was appointed the first African member of the Executive Council.

In the same year, the Colonial Secretary increased the number of official members in the Legco to 26 and that of unofficial members to 28. Of these, six Africans and 1 Arab were nominated and six Indians and 14 Europeans were elected.

In 1954, the Colonial Secretary came to Kenya and held constitutional talks which changed the Executive Council into the Council of Ministers. Two years later, more Africans were nominated to the Legco. This raised their number to eight. Two others were nominated from the Board of Commerce, Agriculture and Trade to sit on the Legco. The Council of Ministers was also increased by two more unofficial members. This included one African and one European who were appointed to that post basically on merit.

Africans had by now become very politically conscious and aware of their role in the constitutional and political development of their country. They demanded that African representation in the Legco be increased to 15. This prompted Mr Lennox-Boyd, who had succeeded Oliver Lyttelton as Colonial Secretary, to go to Kenya for another round of constitutional talks. As a result of these talks, the Lyttelton constitution was scrapped in 1958 and replaced with the Lennox-Boyd constitution. According to the new constitution:

(i) The number of the elected African members was to be increased to 16.

(ii) 4 non-Muslim Asians were to be elected members.

(iii) 2 Muslim Asians were also to be elected members.

(iv) 2 Arabs were to be elected to represent the interests of the Arabs.

(v) The Governor was to nominate 12 specially elected members who would include 4 Africans, 4 Europeans and 4 Asians.

In 1959, the elected African members rejected the Lennox-Boyd constitution. This led to the constitutional conference of 1960 called by Macleod, the new Colonial Secretary. This conference was held in Lancaster House in London and recommended the following:

(i) The Legislative Council was to consist of 65 elected members, of whom 53 would be directly elected while twelve others are elected by the members of the Legislative Council and called national members.

(ii) The Governor reserved the right to appoint three Ministers and the Speaker of the Legislative Council.

(iii) The right to vote be restricted.

(iv) The Council of Ministers should become the Executive Council. And this Council would comprise 4 Africans, 3 Europeans and 1 Asian.

A second constitutional meeting was held in Lancaster House in 1962. It recommended that representatives to the Legislative Council should be elected from every district. These representatives would constitute the Upper House. While other representatives were to be elected from various constituencies by universal adult suffrage. The Council of Ministers would form the Lower House.

In 1963, elections were held as recommended by the Lancaster constitutional conference. Jomo Kenyatta became the first Prime Minister with full powers and on 12th December 1963, Kenya became completely independent.

34

Political development in Kenya

The white settlers, led by aggressive men such as Colonel Grogan and Lord Delamere, were the first people to organise themselves into a political group. By 1911, the settlers had already formed an association. In 1920, the settlers were granted the right to elect 11 members to the Legislative Council (Legco). No other racial group enjoyed this privilege. The aim was simply to make Kenya a settler-dominated self-governing colony. The settlers were not satisfied with direct representation in the Legco. They did not want to accept equality with other races in Kenya. They opposed the Asian demand for equality and demanded that Asian immigration into Kenya should be restricted. They also insisted that schools and hospitals be segregated.

All these settler demands caused a lot of anger among the Asians who sent delegations to London to plead with the Duke of Devonshire for justice. The problem was solved by issuing the Devonshire White Paper. The white settlers' racial demands were not limited to the Asians. They objected to Africans' participation in cash crop production. This, according to them, would lead to the production of substandard crops and would also reduce the supply of labour to the white settler farms.

Asians

The Asians, who mostly lived in urban centres, developed their own cultural and social organisations. Under the East Africa Indian National Congress, they obtained support from the British government in India. Among the prominent Indian leaders in East Africa was Jeevanjee.

The Indians demanded equality with the white settlers. They also strongly demanded the right to settle in the Kenya highlands which were reserved entirely for the white settlers.

235

However, the Indians did not achieve their objectives, partly because they did not try to win African support in the struggle against settler domination.

Africans

The Africans in Kenya became politically conscious earlier than their counterparts in Tanganyika and Uganda. This was largely because of the following reasons:

- The Africans had a common enemy, the white settlers who had been encouraged by the British government to take over their land and subject them to forced labour.

- The Africans from all regions of Kenya had the same grievances. These were based on land alienation, forced labour and heavy taxation.

- The whites in Kenya wished to reduce the Africans to the status of slaves. This strengthened African political unity and led to the formation of some African organisations to counter the dangers of white domination.

African political opinion did not, however, make itself felt until the 1920s when, as a result of World War I and closer contacts with European culture and life, various groups were formed to press home their aspirations. At first these groups were tribal and local, and their demands were moderate.

In 1920, the Kikuyu Association was formed. It consisted of a number of chiefs and headmen. It was led by Chief Koinange, an appointee of the government. Owing to its moderate stance, many people were disatisfied with the Kikuyu Association. Accordingly, in 1921, a more militant group called the Young Kikuyu Association was formed. It was led by a dynamic young man, Harry Thuku.

The members of the Young Kikuyu Association demanded:

(a) The withdrawal of the *kipande* (identity card) that all Africans were legally required to carry.

(b) The reduction of poll tax.
(c) Better labour conditions.
(c) The return of Kikuyu land.

In order to articulate these demands, Thuku addressed large African gatherings in Kavirondo and Kikuyuland. The Kikuyu Association denounced the actions of the Young Kikuyu Association. The government arrested Thuku and deported him to Kismayu. The Association was left leaderless and it continued under the name of Kikuyu Central Association. But the association had lost steam.

In 1922, a group of young "graduates" of the Church Missionary Society's school at Maseno formed the Young Kavirondo Association. The main concern was the danger of land alienation; they feared that part of their land might be appropriated. They were also opposed to the system of kipande and the heavy taxation. In 1923, a missionary archdeacon changed the name of the association to Kavirondo Taxpayers Welfare Association and the group lost its meaning.

In 1928, a Scottish missionary provoked the Kikuyu Central Association by trying to stamp out the custom of female circumcision among the Kikuyu. The association rose up to defend the customs of its people against alien influence. Prominent in this controversy was Jomo Kenyatta. He was the editor of the Kikuyu Central Association newspaper, *Miugwithania*, and also the General Secretary of the association. The clash between the Kikuyu Central Association and the church was a turning point. Many private schools shot up in Kikuyuland to counter the influence of the missionary schools which were out to destroy the African culture especially in Kikuyuland. These schools gradually produced the most outspoken critics of the Europeans and of colonial rule.

Much of the political activity was centred in Kikuyuland because the Kikuyu were the ones most directly involved in controversies over land and also because they were closest to the heartland of European influence, Nairobi. Other African organisations which were opposed to white domination were formed during the 1930s. These associations included the Kavirondo Association, formed by the Baluhya as a response to land alienation; the Ukamba Members' Association which was formed primarily to object to the government destocking campaign in Kambaland. It is worth noting that although all these associations were formed by people of different backgrounds and ages, they shared the same nationalist ambitions.

Towards the outbreak of the Second World War, the Kikuyu Central Association became very popular because it had sent a petition to Britain demanding that:

(a) the Africans be allowed to grow coffee,

(b) the Kikuyu be governed by one Paramount Chief,

(c) the Kenya laws be published in the Kikuyu language, and

(d) Harry Thuku be released.

All their petitions were sent by Johnstone Kamau, who was later to become known as Jomo Kenyatta. However, in the course of the war, the Kikuyu Central Association was banned along with all allied associations in Kenya such as the Kikuyu Association and the Kikuyu Central Taxpayers Association. Mr James Gichuru, who was one of the founders of the Kenya African Study Union (KASU), convened a meeting of the KASU members at which it was proposed to change the name of the association to the Kenya African Union (KAU) in 1946. James Gichuru became president of KAU.

Jomo Kenyatta

In September of the same year Jomo Kenyatta returned from England. In June 1947, he replaced James Gichuru as president of KAU. Jomo Kenyata's immediate challenge was how to weld together people beyond Kikuyuland under the Kenya African Union and thus turn it into a strong political party. Though a very large number of Kenyans were illiterate, Jomo Kenyatta still managed to weld together the Africans under the Kenya African Association. Kenyatta met a lot of hostility from the Europeans who demanded that he should be deported.

Mau Mau rebellion

Some members of the Kenya African Union in 1948 had formed the Kenya Land and Freedom Army, a militant and very radical group which resorted to arms in 1951 in what is known as Mau Mau to drive the white settlers away from their land.

The words 'Mau Mau' mean different things to different people. According to the sympathisers of the colonialists, Mau Mau was a barbaric, backward and anti-European tribal cult whose leaders had planned to pull Kenya from the direction of progress to that of darkness and death. Some of them defined it as a movement designed to impose the dominance of the Kikuyu tribe on the entire Kenyan people. However, according to the African historian, B.A. Ogot, Mau Mau was a desperate attempt by a desperate people to change a system of economic and social injustice which is a marked feature of Kenyan history.

All in all, the Mau Mau movement was an active nationalist force whose organisers had set out to resist the oppression of alien rulers.

Causes of Mau Mau

Several factors contributed in different proportions to the Mau Mau revolt.

- One of the immediate causes of the Mau Mau was the Second World War. Africans who had participated in the war had gone through a lot of experiences, such that they now wanted immediate independence.

- Careless utterances of the white settlers. For instance, in 1950 a prominent settler announced: "We are here to stay and the other races must accept that fact with all that it implies." This was annoying to the nationalists who no longer wanted to be slaves of the white men.

- The population pressure in Central Kenya also caused the Mau Mau movement. Many people were deprived of their land and concentrated within land reserves which, unfortunately, did not yield enough food to feed the growing population. Land alienation in the highlands had generated a lot of discontent.

- The Europeans made a grave mistake of evicting African squatters from settler farms. These squatters were pushed into overpopulated reserves where there were no jobs or land. All this suffering made the Africans look at violence as the only means of salvaging themselves from the unfair treatment meted out to them by the Europeans.

- The high cost of living in Kenya. For instance, between 1949 and 1952, the cost of living rose by 40 percent while weekly wages rose from sh 7/62 to sh 14/13 only. The high cost of living forced the Africans to demand better wages.

- Racial discrimination by the white settlers. The Africans were discriminated against with regard to employment, salaries, hotels, sports, growing coffee, etc.

Initially, Mau Mau was not taken seriously. In 1948, when government was investigating cases of intimidation of the Kikuyu squatters, Governor Phillip Mitchell underrated the power of the Mau Mau. He thought the movement was a mere cult. By 1950, African leaders were already impatient and they wanted the number of Africans in the Legislative Council to be increased. One member of KAU demanded that independence should be granted within three years.

As the Europeans hesitated, matters were gradually getting out of hand. Acts of violence had aroused fear in the settlers, who called for government action. In 1951 Mau Mau was declared an unlawful society and its leaders took refuge in the forests, chiefly in the Aberdare and Mt Kenya areas. In October 1952, Senior Chief Waruhiu was murdered in cold blood for his loyalty to government. This made the Europeans realise the gravity of the situation. A State of Emergency was immediately declared. Kenyatta and many other KAU leaders were arrested and charged with organising and supporting the wave of violence. Kenyatta was found guilty and sentenced to seven years' imprisonment in 1953.

In June 1953, KAU was banned for four years, but the war continued and it took a heavy toll on both the Europeans and the Africans. The Mau Mau fighters were only weakened when their topmost leaders, General China and Dedan Kimathi, were arrested. Despite these setbacks, Mau Mau activities continued around the Aberdares until 1956. In 1960, the State of Emergency was lifted.

Consequences of Mau Mau

- The war cost the lives of about 10,000 Mau Mau men, 2,000 Kikuyu civilians, 1,000 government troops and 58 civilians, both European and Asian.

- The Mau Mau forced tens of thousands of people into reserves and detention camps where there was human suffering and horror.

- Thousands of prisoners suffered harsh treatment and poor living conditions.

- Terror and fear of death was the order of the day for many people for many years.

- African solidarity, which existed in clans and tribes, weakened as some members of the same clan or tribe were seen as traitors because of their loyalty to the whites.

- Britain and Kenya lost about fifty million pounds in the war.

- The Mau Mau rebellion demonstrated to the constitutional planners that majority rule was inevitable.

- It also revealed to the Europeans that they could not control the internal situation in Kenya.

- The white settlers and the Africans realised that the responsibility for a permanent settlement rested with Britain.

- The Mau Mau also taught the British to respect the opinion of the African leaders. As a result, power shifted from the hands of the settlers to the Africans.

- It also forced the government to create a consistent policy towards African participation in the governance of Kenya:

the number of Africans nominated to take part in government was increased to more than five.

- It encouraged the government to effect constitutional changes in 1954, 1957 and 1960 in order to bring about stability and racial harmony.

- The Mau Mau also popularised imprisoned KAU leaders such as Jomo Kenyatta.

- The Mau Mau rebellion taught different races to coexist.

After the Mau Mau, the speed of both political and constitutional advance became rapid. As we have already seen in the previous chapter, in 1954, the Colonial Secretary, Oliver Lyttelton visited Kenya and produced a plan for a multi-racial Council of Ministers to replace the Executive Council. The unofficial members included one African, two Asians and three Europeans.

Some extremist Europeans, led by one Captain Briggs, criticised Lyttelton's reform. They did not accept a multi-racial government; they wanted white domination to continue in Kenya. In 1955, the ban on political parties was lifted and parties allowed to function at local level. This promoted the rise of new leaders, and by 1958, people like Tom Mboya, Oginga Odinga, Daniel arap Moi, Ronald Ngala, Jeremiah Nyagah and Dr Julius Kiano had become members of the Legco. It was not until the famous 'wind of change' speech by the British Prime Minister, Macmillan, that the whites realised that Kenya was no longer going to be the white man's country.

In 1959, the African members of the Legco boycotted the council and demanded a constitutional conference. Since Jomo Kenyatta was the only one able to unite all the Africans, they also demanded his release from prison.

In January 1960, a constitutional conference took place in Lancaster House in London. After a month of discussions, there was still strong disagreement between Ngala and Mboya on the one hand and Captain Brigg's group on the other. They, however, agreed on the following:

(i) The 12 specially elected members were to remain.

(ii) There were to be 33 open seats.

(iii) There were to be 20 reserved seats (2 Arabs, 8 Asians and 10 Europeans).

(iv) The Council of Ministers would consist of 8 unofficial members (4 Africans, 1 Asian and 3 Europeans) and four official members.

The Africans accepted this as a temporary arrangement. They now had a majority on the unofficial side of the Legislative Council and some control over the reserved seats.

The Europeans in Kenya were alarmed and some of them started selling their property, while others demanded compensation from Britain so that they could sell their farms and leave Kenya.

In 1960, a new national party, the Kenya African National Union (KANU), was formed by African leaders in the Legislative Council. Mr Gichuru was its president, Mr Odinga Oginga its vice president and Mr Mboya its general secretary. This party was very radical, and it was mainly urban-centred.

This forced the other leaders to form the Kenya African Democratic Union (KADU) in 1960 with the support of the Kalenjin, the Maasai, the people of northern Nyanza and the coast. Its leaders were Ngala, Masinde Muliro and Daniel arap Moi. KADU advocated a federal constitution which would pre-empt the domination of Kenya by the Luo and Kikuyu through KANU. In the 1961 elections, while KANU won 19 seats, KADU won eleven. African support for European reserved seats largely went to Blundell's moderates.

KANU was called upon to form a government but it refused on the grounds that Jomo Kenyatta had not yet been released from prison. Mr Ngala was then called upon to lead a government with KADU support.

When Jomo Kenyatta was released from jail in August 1961, he tried to reconcile KANU and KADU, but his efforts were not successful. He therefore became president of KANU.

In 1962, a constitutional conference was again held in Lancaster House in London. It was hoped that the differences between KADU and KANU would be ironed out. Some members of KANU joined the government and a constitution was drawn up.

In the elections of May 1963 KANU won 85 seats and KADU only 41. On 1sh June 1963, Jomo Kenyatta became prime minister with full powers of internal self-government. Many opposition members joined the government and Jomo Kenyatta chose his ministers from many different communities. The constitution was again changed to reduce the powers of regions. Kenya became independent on 12th December 1963 and Mzee Jomo Kenyatta became the first president of the Republic of Kenya.

35

Closer union in East Africa

The idea of closer union of East Africa was contemplated as early as 1898. When Johnston came to Uganda in 1899, he had it in mind. Charles Eliot also shared the same idea. He believed that the longer Kenya and Uganda stayed apart, the more divergent their policies would become and it would be difficult to merge them later. When Britain acquired Tanganyika after the First World War, the idea of merging the three territories became more popular. In 1922, Winston Churchill, the British Colonial Secretary, declared that he looked forward to the federation of East Africa, a hope which was also shared by his successor, L.S. Amery, in 1924.

In 1924, a commission of inquiry was appointed under the chairmanship of the Honourable W. Ormsby-Gome to find out the possibility of forging a federation. He found out the following.

Uganda

In Uganda strong feelings against federation were expressed by Baganda leaders. They opposed it on the grounds that this would interfere with their special position as set out in the 1900 Buganda Agreement. They also feared white domination which was already evident in the Kenya highlands.

Hatred of the federation in Uganda came up clearly in 1953 when the then colonial secretary made reference to the possibility of an East African federation. There was an immediate outcry which led to the deportation of the Kabaka.

Kenya

Originally, the idea of closer union was opposed by both Africans and the white settlers. The Africans thought that

245

The white settlers hoped to benefit a great deal from the federation provided they had a say in the government and the shaping of its policies. They therefore became strong supporters of the federation.

When Sir Edward Grigg was appointed Governor of Kenya he was instructed to design plans for the federation. His committee recommended the implementation of the plan in 1927.

Tanganyika

Here the opinion was not in favour of union. The first outspoken critic of the system was the Governor, Sir Donald Cameron. He had been angered by the actions of the governors of Uganda and Kenya in trying to stop the building of the railway link between Tabora and Mwanza, which would inevitably take away some of the trade and traffic that went through Uganda and Kenya. Cameron threatened to resign if the plan was carried out. The British government also got concerned since Tanganyika was a mandate territory and as such it had to cater for the welfare of the Africans. So most people in Tanganyika were not in favour of the federation at all.

Though there was a lot of opposition from various communities against federation, the British government did not give up the idea. In 1928, another commission was set up. This was the Hilton Young Commission. It found out that a complete political federation was not viable, but recommended that a High Commissioner for East Africa should be appointed with powers to control the policies affecting the populations of East Africa. This recommendation came to nothing since the settlers did not support it.

The idea of federation was dropped in the 1930s. It had, however, been made clear that there was a possibility of closer union in the field of economic and social affairs and it was along these lines that the Governors' conference developed. From 1930 they met regularly.

An East African Currency Board had been set up by 1920 and by 1930 railways, customs, defence, posts and telegraphs were shared at least between Kenya and Uganda. All the three territories came to adopt common tariffs and to standardise policies on African taxation, elementary education, communications and industry. During the Second World War, a joint Economic Council for East and Central Africa was set up, with a Secretariat, to share resources available and contribute towards the war. Many other bodies were set up to deal with research, supplies and refugees, but they did not outlast the war.

Formation of East Africa High Commission

The East Africa High Commission was established in 1948 with its headquarters in Nairobi. The commission consisted of the three governors of East Africa, together with an executive organisation headed by a commissioner, and a legislative body with powers to make laws affecting the common services of the three countries.

The members of the legislative body were to be chosen by the three countries on a racial basis. Some were to be elected while others were to be nominated. The powers of the commission were limited. It had no revenue of its own but depended on grants from the three member states. Neither did it have an army, a police force, law courts or power to enforce laws of its own apart from the regulations mentioned above.

Functions of the Commission

In spite of the limitations imposed upon it, the commission proved to be an effective and useful body. It combined and co-ordinated a wide range of functions. The commission played a great role in the development of the East African railways and harbours. It also promoted East African posts and telecommunications. The commission also controlled

East African leaders discussing formation of East Africa High Commission

customs and excise. This led to the development of the East African customs and excise department. Furthermore, the commission promoted higher education which led to the development of Makerere College, which was the highest institution of learning in East Africa at that time.

It also helped in setting up the East African income tax department, defence and civil aviation directorates, and research institutions. The commission also set up the East African Literature Bureau to contribute to the development of the publishing sector. In 1961, the High Commission became the East African Common Services Organisation. It continued successfully to encourage economic development.

After independence each country, however, went its separate way and followed its own path of development.

Revision 29, 30, 31, 32, 33, 34 & 35

1 What was the contribution of the following to Tanganyika's struggle for independence?

(a) Tanganyika African National Union (TANU)

(b) Sir Richard Turnbull

2 (a) Explain the causes of the Mau Mau rebellion.

(b) How was Kenya affected by the rebellion up to independence?

3 (a) What problems did political parties in East Africa face before independence?

(b) Describe the achievements of either the Uganda People's Congress (UPC) or the Kenya African National Union (KANU) by 1965.

4 (a) What led to the Declaration of the Devonshire White Paper of 1923?

(b) What were the terms of the Devonshire White Paper?

5 (a) Why was East Africa involved in World War II?

(b) How did the war affect the growth of nationalism in East Africa?

6 (a) What attempts were made to bring about closer union between the East African territories between 1926 and 1960?

(b) Why did the attempt fail?

7 (a) What factors contributed to the growth of nationalism in East Africa between 1945 and 1960?

(b) Describe the difficulties faced by the nationalists.

8 Describe Jomo Kenyatta's career and his contribution to the development of his country up to independence.

9 (a) How did World War II contribute to the growth of nationalism in Kenya?

(b) What problems did African Kenyans face in their struggle for independence?

10 Describe the political and economic activities of the white settlers in Kenya up to 1945.

11 (a) Why was there no national political party in Uganda until 1952?

(b) What contribution did the Uganda National Congress (UNC) make towards the struggle for independence in Uganda?

12 (a) What were the causes of the Kabaka Crisis of 1953-55?

Index

Abaluhya, 10
Abatembuzi, 38
Abolition of slave trade, 97-101
Acholi, 7
Adhola, 7
Alur, 6
Anglo-German Agreement 1886, 130-131
Ankole Agreement 1901, 140
Arabs, 15

Babito dynasty, 7, 42
Bachwezi, 13, 39-42
Baganda, 10
Bahima, 48
Bairu, 48
Baker, Sir Samuel, 107-108, 126-127
Bantu, 2, 10-11
Banyankore, 10
Banyarwanda, 10
Banyoro, 10
Bar-el-Ghazel, 5
Bataka system, 42
Berlin conference, 130
British protectorate, 123, 134
British rule, response of
      Nandi, 158-159
      Maasai, 157
Buganda, 50-55, 133-134
Buganda Agreement 1900, 123, 136-140
Bunyoro-Kitara, 37-44, 140-141
Burton, 105
Busoga, 7

Captain Frederick Lugard, 133-140
Caucasoid race, 2
Chagga, 10, 64-65
Christianity, 25, 102
Church Missionary Society (CMS), 103-105

Colonial rule
      Eastern Uganda, 141-144
      Northern Uganda, 144-146
Constitutional development in
      Kenya, 232-235
      Uganda, 212-215
      Tanganyika, 227-231
d'Almeida, Francisco, 26
East African coast, 15
East African High Commission, 248-249
Egyptians, 15
Egyptian imperialism, 126-128
Explorers, 105-111
Food crops, 12, 13
Fort Jesus, 19
German East Africa (see Tanganyika)
German East Africa Company (GEA Co.), 121-122, 160
Gipir (Nyipir), 6
Goa, 28
Gogo, 10
Gordon, Charles, 127-128
Greek traders, 15
Hehe, 68
Heligoland Treaty 1890, 133
Ibn Batuta, 18
Imperial British East Africa Company (IBEA Co.), 120-121, 160
Imperialists, 123-125
Indian Ocean trade, 15
Indirect rule in Uganda, 174-178
Iron-working, 13
Islam, 16, 21-23, 102
Iteso, 3, 4, 13
Jie, 4
Johnston, H.H. 123
Jok-Omolo, 6, 7
Jopadhola, 6, 7
Jomo Kenyatta, 239
Kabaka, 50

Kabaka Mutesa, 107
Kabaka Yekka (KY), 218
Kabalega, 43, 126, 150-153
Kagwa, Apollo, 148-149
Kakungulu, Semei, 141-144
Kalenjin group of tribes, 3
Kamurasi, 43
Karagwe, 44-46
Karimojong, 3, 4, 13
Katikkiro, 52
Kenya, 122, 155-159, 206-211
Kenya African National Union
(KANU), 233-235, 244-245
Khedive Ismail, 110
Kikuyu, 10, 65-68
Kilwa, 16, 17
King Leopold II, 155
Kintu, 50
Kipsigis, 3
Kiswahili, 16
Koranic schools, 22
Krapf, Dr Ludwig, 103
Kumam, 4
Kwavi, 61-64

Labongo, 6
Langi, 5
Lango, 7
Legislative Council (Legco), 212-215
Livingstone, Dr David, 108-109
Long-distance trade, 92-101
Lukiiko, 212-215
Luo speaking peoples, 5-9
Mackinnon, William, 120-121
Makonde, 10
Malindi, 19, 28
Maasai, 3, 13, 59-61
Mau Mau, 240-244
Mazruis, 33-34
Mbaguta, Nuwa, 149-150
Meru, 10
Migration, 1, 2, 4, 10
Mirambo, 76-78
Missionaries, 102, 112-117
Mkwawa, 80-81

Mogadishu, 16, 17
Mombasa, 16, 18
Monomotapa, 71
Mozambique, 28
Mumia, Nabongo, 156-157
Munyigumba, 80
Musaazi, Ignatius, 218
Nandi, 3, 57-59
Nationalist movements in Uganda,
217-218
Ngoni, 11, 70-74
Nilotes, 2, 3
Nkore, 47-48
Ntemi chiefdom, 56-57
Nyamwezi, 56-57
Nyanza province, Kenya, 7
Nyungu ya Mawe, 78
Obote, Apollo Milton, 219-222
Oman, 32-36

Pasha, Emin, 134
Pastoralists, 4, 5, 13
Pemba, 17, 19
Persians, 16
Peters, Karl, 121, 124-125, 155, 160
Pokot, 3
Political development in
        Kenya, 236-244
        Uganda, 216-226
        Tanganyika, 227-231
Portuguese, 18, 24-31
Prophet Muhammed, 21
Resistance to German rule and
occupation
        Abushiri revolt, 161-164
        Hehe resistance, 164-165
        Maji Maji uprising, 181-186
        Makonde, 165
        Unyanyembe, 166
Rhodes, Cecil, 124
Royal Geographical Society, 105
Rugaruga, 76
Rwot Awich 153-154
Samburu, 3
Sayyid Said, 82, 103
Saza chiefs, 43

Scramble for and partition of East Africa, 128-130
Shariah law, 17
Shirazi dynasty, 17
Shifting cultivation, 13
Slave trade, 92-101, 133
Slavery, 92
Sofala, 17, 25
Southern Nyanza, 7
Speke, 105-107
Stanley, Henry Morton, 110
Sultan of Zanzibar, 155
Swahili, 18, 22,
Tanganyika, 122, 160-166, 180-186, 190-196
Tanganyika African Union (TANU), 226, 228-231
The land of Zenj, 16
Toro Agreement 1900, 140
Trade items, 15
Turkana, 3, 4, 13
Turks, 25
Uganda, 122, 133-146, 197-205
Uganda National Congress (UNC), 218-219
Uganda People's Congress (UNC), 219-222
Uganda Railway, 122, 170-173
Unyamwezi, 76
Unyanyembe, 79-80
Vasco da Gama, 24
West Nile, 7
World War I, 187-189
Zanzibar, 19
Zanzibar under the British, 167-169
Zwangendaba, 70, 71